MW01481953

FORECLOSURE

Ethical Foreclosure Investing Strategies for Massive Wealth Creation

PROFIT MACHINE

TJ Marrs

Outskirts Press, Inc.
Denver, Colorado

Foreclosure Profit Machine
Ethical Foreclosure Investing Strategies for Massive Wealth Creation

Outskirts Press
http://www.outskirtspress.com

ISBN 10: 1-59800-212-0
ISBN 13: 978-1-59800-212-6

Printed in the United States of America

Disclaimer

The information in this educational manual is designed to provide accurate and authoritative information in regard to the subject matter covered. It is offered with the understanding that the presenters are not engaged in rendering legal, accounting, or other professional service. If legal advice or other expert advice is required, the services of a competent professional should be sought.

Adapted from a Declaration of Principals jointly adopted by a committee of the American Bar Association and a Committee of Publishers and Associations.

Table of Contents

About the Author

T.J. Marrs has performed hundreds of real estate transactions as a licensed California Real Estate Agent, an Oregon & Washington licensed Mortgage Broker & Mortgage Banker, and a real estate investor over the past 17 years. T.J. has also held professional certifications in securities and insurance. He is a decorated U.S. Naval Intelligence Officer who served during the Iran-Iraq War and the Cold War.

While parking his car to attend Midnight Mass on Christmas 1998, T.J. survived a near-fatal multiple stabbing attack in a church parking lot. Ever since then, T.J. has dedicated his life to helping others overcome their fears and obstacles so they can change their lives. T. J. has authored two books and multiple courses on real estate and is developing another on business success. He currently serves as Chairman of the Northwest Real Estate Investors Association. He now dedicates his time to his real estate investments, speaking internationally, and helping his students succeed in their businesses. He is the select author for one of the internet's highest volume web sites on Real Estate, RealtyTrac.com. He has twice been interviewed by the Wall Street Journal and CNBC's Power Lunch. He has also contributed to "The Idiots Guide to Foreclosure Investing" and "House Poor" (Harper Collins).

T.J.'s motto is "Helping people succeed, one person at a time." T.J. invites everyone to try his success newsletter, available at: www.tjmarrs.com

T.J. Marrs
www.tjmarrs.com

Foreword

Homeownership today is at an all-time high. Every American wants to own his or her own home. At least, those who understand the value of owning their own home do.

At an unprecedented level, our government is providing incentives to own homes. The banking system is offering record level low rates to entice people to become homeowners. This all began during the period following World War II, when the government made it a priority to provide housing for returning veterans. President Roosevelt created this program for the veterans so that they would receive better treatment and benefits in exchange for their service to the country. These measures eventually led to the GI Bill and the Federal Housing Administration (FHA). These events have caused a mass movement and understanding of the opportunity to own your own home.

Rather than live in poorly designed and cramped apartments with little economic opportunity or pride, homeownership gave Americans the dream of building their own little nest egg, which they could eventually use during retirement. We have long seen homeownership as a tool to provide community pride and improve the social condition of our entire society. These opportunities, combined with the postwar economic boom, affected the Baby Boomer generation. This entire generation has grown up with a higher standard and has really had to deal with the harsh economic conditions of the prior generation. Homeownership in a nicer place is an expectation, not just an opportunity to expand one's life.

As the demand for homes stays high, and the government and financial markets create sources of cheap loans, the economy has grown to record levels. Thus, we have seen amazing prosperity during these past 50 years.

Through all of the interest rate fluctuations, people still want to own their own home. Of course, they want it at the cheapest price possible. However, prices in some areas of the country have risen significantly faster than incomes can rise. When interest rates rise, this has a further impact on what we call the "affordability index." Other factors, such as the rising cost of living, inflation, oil prices, and the effect of over-borrowing money, can significantly impact one's lifestyle. This is the basis for the fear of a "housing bubble."

However, in reality, the only places to worry about such conditions are in the super high-end markets, which have seen the fastest appreciation in recent years. That is a market-by-market concern, not a national one. What goes up fast just might come crashing down fast. On the other hand, as long as demand is high, I believe housing is a great place to invest, as long as you have the right buying strategies and criteria.

As far as foreclosure investments are concerned, we can make money in any market. If the market is up, consumers tend to over-buy and therefore overextend themselves. When a market is down, there is a general trend of more foreclosures in that market. We simply adjust our buying and selling strategies to fit the marketplace. As long as people need a place to live, we are in business. What a great business this is. More importantly, we are actually helping these people improve their situations and avoid a credit catastrophe that could ruin their futures.

Another condition that creates a solid marketplace for a foreclosure investor is the tendency for Americans to borrow too much. Then, something happens which disrupts their ability to pay. In some cases, people are simply credit abusers. In other cases, it is just bad luckthat leads to a distressed seller situation. Our society has actually evolved into one of "indentured servitude." This means that we live our lives around paying our bills, living from paycheck to paycheck. As a result, some of us fail. The good news is we live in a great country where anyone can recover, if they make the effort.

My Goal for This Book

I, for one, don't believe indentured servitude is a way to live, but merely a slow way to die. One of my goals in writing this book is to educate consumers about this reality and to educate people as to how this reality creates opportunity at the same time. I'm not suggesting one take advantage of people in distress, but merely to recognize how to help others improve their situation, while improving your situation at the same time. You really can get into the real estate investing business and build a fortune. It takes hard work, plus the mentality that you are building a real business.

Purchasing foreclosures is by no means an easy answer to lowering your cost of living or to venturing into a new business of real estate investing. I want to encourage you to be a real estate investor and a better consumer.

My motto has always been:

"You're automatically already in the real estate business. The real question is, 'Are you profiting from it, or are you the one providing the profit to someone else?' With this training, you have the opportunity to make that choice."

Everyone relies on real estate to exist on this planet. From the beginning of time, human beings have fought and died over real estate concerns. Today, corporations rely on it for major portions of their holdings. Stocks come and go, but the real estate stays and generally continues to increase in value.

For this reason, I also tell my students who are considering this business:

"Real estate is the business of all businesses."

One simple objective of this book is to give you an introduction to the idea of purchasing a home at a discount. Another is to show you some great strategies that can help you increase your profits as a real estate investor, even if you don't have a lot of time, money, or credit.

If you are a Realtor, my hope is that you will look at this business from the point of view of the consumer and the investor to see ways in which you could expand your business. Many realtors get into the business with the intent of becoming investors, only to find out later that they're in a different business than real investors. Real estate licensing school does little to teach you how to invest the way I can. So, I hope this book can help you get closer to the dreams you had.

Good luck, and happy hunting.

T.J. Marrs

What have students said about TJ's materials and support...

I like the practical examples and hands on instruction.

A comprehensive, practical course combining excepts and actions to make them real. Thanks. *Fred M.*

The way T.J. presented his information in a local format. I feel I can get started without being scared, because I will know how to focus on one step at a time and not worry about the unknown. P.S. I have attended other seminars and have always come away overwhelmed and have not taken any action! With T.J's coaching I an excited to get started and am looking forward to taking action. *Lisa R.*

...This student found his first deal within 3 weeks for a profit of almost $30,000.....I almost negotiated the deal for a $10,000 profit, TJ showed me how to find another $20,000 I never realized I could get out of the deal on my own. *Casey C.*

...I did not believe you at first. Who would sell to us with such terms? Somebody would give their home away!? I thought it was just a once in a life time chance. In my first month I made $10,000 and it only took me a total of 10 hours of work. More recently I acquired new TWO more deals with no money out of pocket, with over $85,000 in combined equity! *Chris B.*

I pulled $55,000 cash out at my purchase closing on first deal with T.J. *Steven M.*

I am already wholesaling an average of 4 transactions a month, with a wholesale profit of about $2,000-$3000 cash each deal. With your help I am sure I will be able to perfect my deals so they become more profitable. *Oscar M.*

...I am very grateful we have had the opportunity to work together and become friends. By following your suggestions I have been able to create a bright future for myself. I am very excited about this. I realize I don't have to stay stuck in a j.o.b for the rest of my life. I realize I have the personality and drive to be successful, but I know many people are not risk takers and may not take enough action to change their lives. I tried to say something today to motivate the people in your training. *Leaha L.*

I've always heard: "them's that can... do; them's that can't... teach." It's good to find someone who can, and teaches! *Jess Jessup.*

I have one deal complete and 5 others started (that's over $1m in properties).

"You have made real estate investing processes so easy to understand, given the multitude of marketing tips, and new time saving auto forms, makes the investor more confident about the paperwork. You've done it all for us, except talk to the motivated sellers (and the new CD of TJ talking to sellers does that too)."

"I have been looking for a program s comprehensive as this for years. I would highly recommend this course for anyone that is serious about operating a real estate investment business!" *Debbie T.*

You're too good!! You REALLY do want us to succeed don't you??:-)) Thank you very much, TJ. *Briana W.*

I definitely know I am exactly where I need to be (with your program). I continue to go through your course and find that it is as complete as a course could be. Thank you for that . **Scott S.**

Thank you for your reply and the e-book . I just finished the 45 minute audio and all I can say is WOW !!! It appears you have been doing this for a long time. You did lose me on the whole trust thing at the end of the audio but most of the rest I could comprehend. **Jason.**

I took the "$5,000 in 15 Days Challenge" program after last Wednesday's (11/17) call and I'm just writing to tell you that tomorrow, Sunday 11/22/04, I am going to meet with 2 sellers on 2 properties!

Property 1 was actually taken sub2 by another local investor who has too many projects going and she wants to pass it on. She's already even gotten 5 or 6 potential tenant buyers for the property. All I have to do is pay her an assignment fee (which I can get from a portion of the TB's option payment) and the place will be mine (or rather, my TB's!).

Property 2 is a pre-foreclosure. The owner is willing to just walk away, basically. She's 3 months behind, owes $256k and the property is worth approx. $280k. Might take this one over for myself! It's a nice place on 5 acres. Or maybe I'll flip it to a retail buyer, leaving them some built in equity so that I can move it fast and walk away with $12k or so.

Any tips or advice on these would greatly appreciated. Thanks for your course, TJ. It's down to earth, practical and well laid out. I love the fact it came with all the forms, too!
Take care, **Annie Anderson**

Thank you for helping me reach my peak potential as a real estate investor. **Lonnie Wiig**

CHAPTER 1
Introduction: What is a Foreclosure?

Foreclosure seems to be one of today's hot money making phrases, one that is frankly overused by the "get rich quick overnight" gurus. I am not indicating that you cannot get rich with foreclosure real estate. You can. But first, we must gain a realistic understanding of what foreclosure is and learn some basic terminology required to develop in this business.

"Foreclosure" simply means to stop or prevent an event, a term we usually associate with real estate. A more legal approach to this issue is, to stop a borrower from his right to redeem the property. In a typical mortgage arrangement, the borrower is referred to as the "mortgagor." The lender is referred to as the "mortgagee." These terms are more common in the states that use a mortgage instrument, versus those states that use a trust deed. The borrower "gives a mortgage" and the lender receives the contract for it. In exchange, the lender grants a loan of funds to purchase a property.

The foreclosure process provides a legal means for the lender to exercise its security in the property and take it back, due to nonperformance of payments by the borrower. The property was given as security for the note. Since the note was not performed on, that security is given up. The instrument that is recorded to secure the promissory note is either a trust deed or a mortgage instrument. I commonly refer to this as the "lien instrument" used to secure the mortgage.

Exactly what does a bank do when it gives you a loan?

First of all, the bank lends you money and, in exchange, receives your pledge of the property as security. As the mortgagor, you will give the mortgagee (the bank) a mortgage type instrument in exchange for this privilege. Most people reverse this terminology. Most people believe the bank gave them a mortgage. This is simply not a correct way to look at it. You give the mortgage instrument in exchange for the loan funds. As we proceed, you will come into a clearer understanding of this.

After closing a transaction, the borrower will sign a mortgage or trust deed at closing. At that time, you simultaneously receive, the deed of ownership to the property, as the purchaser. The title officer or closing officer's job is to ensure everything happens as necessary to safely transfer title. The reason an escrow is used is that it is impossible to do everything at the exact same time. Therefore, we use the terms "open escrow" and "closed escrow" to describe the process of completing all the steps of the paperwork. This third party sees to it that everything is completed prior to what we call a "closing." The closing company will also ensure that everything is properly recorded on the county records.

Keep this thought in mind while studying this book. Most of the concepts I'm speaking of are universal in nature, yet can vary from state to state, county to county, and town to town. You can always consult a local adviser, one who is either experienced in the market or is an attorney practicing real estate law in your area.

Another possible source of good information about your local characteristics might be a local Realtor who is familiar with foreclosures in your area. You can also use that same relationship for obtaining values on properties, working short sales (covered later), and many other useful services. Get a good relationship with your local Realtor early on.

Be advised, these people will not necessarily want to give away free advice. You will need to show them what is in it for them. Is there future business? Is there a future fee in it? Is there a free lunch every couple of weeks? Whatever it takes, build these relationships, and they will pay you back many times over.

Other people you might consult about developing your local foreclosure business are:

- Your accountant
- The staff at the county recorder's office
- Other real estate investors
- Local banks who deal with foreclosure properties
- A professional mentor who can be at your call when needed

The difference between a "mortgage" and a "deed of trust" or "trust deed"

Although both instruments perform a similar function, there are slight variations to be aware of. In a trust deed arrangement, a "trustor" (borrower) essentially grants a portion of his legal title on the property to someone called a trustee, who actually becomes the legal title-holder during the obligation of debt. This way, should a foreclosure be necessary, it will be easier to transfer title back to the bank.

In a mortgage method state, there is essentially a lawsuit to get title back. Knowing this, one can understand why more and more banks prefer trust deeds and why more states are going toward trust deeds as the favored instrument. In a trust deed state, a non-judicial procedure is required to process a foreclosure to completion. A "receiver" is essentially appointed to handle this process, should the borrower default and not make the payments as agreed.

As an investor, you should be aware of certain other provisions, which can catch up to you later. The "right of redemption" is a process where the mortgagor has the right to get back the property, even after foreclosure. Watch out for this as an investor. Obviously, some very specific legal requirements must be in place. You would not want to be on the buying side of the transaction and have the mortgagor come back on you. I would not be too concerned with this issue: Just be aware of your local laws. It rarely comes into play. Consult local legal counsel on this.

Common Mortgage Provisions to Be Aware Of

Most savings and loans, banks, and credit unions have certain conditions that must be in place in their mortgage and note instruments.

1. The mortgagor promises to pay back the loan

2. The entire principal will be accelerated and become due should the borrower defaults on payments or tax assessments.

3. Insurance is required to protect the mortgagee's interest.

4. The mortgagor consents to have a receiver appointed in the event of foreclosure.

5. Buildings must remain intact and must not be removed without consent.

6. Many mortgages will also contain a due on sale clause, explained later.

We must always keep in mind that money borrowed is not the borrower's money: It is the lender's. Yes, some people need this explained to them.

The money belonged to the lender. When something is requested as security, that is simply the nature of the lending business.

The provisions that allow the lender to foreclose are built into the process. Having standardized and clearly-understood provisions in place dramatically reduces ambiguity and potential for frivolous lawsuits between the parties.

I should point out that when a foreclosure in a "mortgage state" occurs, there is a effectively a lawsuit filed. A judgment is then given, allowing the lender to take back the property, if needed, to recover their funds. This is an unpleasant and unpredictable process for both parties, which again is why so many states and banks are using trust deeds instead. The trust deed process clearly outlines the process so that it will be fairly automatic without a judicial proceeding. This process is more objective and thus better for both parties, in my opinion.

Avoiding the Foreclosure Auction

In this section, I'm primarily concentrating on the basic subject of foreclosures. You should be aware that there are ways in which the seller facing foreclosure can stop the process, before it is too late. This will come into play if you begin to pursue "pre-foreclosures," as I generally recommend. The best deals to be had are prior to the auction.

Here are a few ways in which an auction can be stopped

- **Forbearance:**

When I am pursuing a property, I want to give the seller every possible positive option, even if I'm not going to purchase property. In such circumstances, I may recommend a forbearance arrangement with the bank. This is simply when the owner of the property works out the repayment arrangement for the back payments due.

For example, there may be $12,000 in back payments due. The lender may allow you to pay $3,000 now and the remaining $9,000 over a period of months, in addition to the regular mortgage payment. This way, the lender can avoid the risks and expense they incur during a foreclosure.

- **Deed in lieu of foreclosure:**

This is essentially when the seller talks to the bank, and they agree that the homeowner will sign over a deed to the property, thereby giving the property back to the bank. Although this might stop foreclosure, it can result in significant credit damage, anyway. Many homeowners believe this will avoid credit problems. This is simply not true.

- **Short sale (How to multiply your profits):**

This is the process of asking for a "discounted payoff" of the current loans. Frequently, lien holders who were in secondary positions on foreclosure properties are at great risk of not receiving any money at all, should the first mortgage lender foreclose. As investors, we will frequently negotiate a small payment to these lenders in exchange for their ownership to the property. Therefore, a great amount of equity can be created for the skilled short sale negotiator.

- **Bring payments current:**

Obviously, this approach requires that all back payments and penalties to be brought current immediately. The lender cannot deny you the right to bring the transaction current. Lenders typically don't like to take partial payments. It is usually all or nothing.

- **Declare bankruptcy:**

Only upon seeking legal counsel, one may decide that bankruptcy is an option. I won't go into detail as to the different types of bankruptcy here, but the mere declaration of bankruptcy can immediately forestall the foreclosure temporary. By itself, it does not automatically prevent foreclosures, though. I have seen bankruptcy used in this way. The homeowner simply files but does not complete the bankruptcy. This can buy a little time, minimize the credit damage, and hold off the foreclosure until an investor can complete the purchasing process.

- **Deed the property to an investor "subject to" existing loans.**

The investor will then make an effort to bring the loan current and pay it off. This one is my favorite methods and thus the most common thing we do.

Each of these choices carries certain credit and financial implications, which should be considered carefully prior to taking the action.

Many of these choices will vary and may be impacted by the available equity in the property. The bottom line is this: If there is a lot of equity, the homeowner has more options regarding refinances, partnerships, leasebacks, or other creative financing arrangements. If there are other liens against the property, these can limit the homeowner and investor options.

As far as credit is concerned, I believe everyone should be concerned with it today. In today's world, to have poor credit is like becoming a second-class citizen for the rest of your life. You'll have to put more money down for more money, you'll pay higher payments and higher interest rates to borrow money, and you'll be looked at in a way that will make you feel uncomfortable for years to come. My biggest pitch to sellers is, "I can help prevent you from being labeled as 'credit criminal' for the next 10 years." I say this not to be cute, but because it is true.

Assuming the auction is looming, now the seller MUST decide what to do...

Borrowers in a pre-foreclosure situation will most likely realize they really will lose their home, equity, credit standing, and that all this will negatively impact their ability to borrow with dignity in the future. This is not a problem easily ignored, as many people in this situation find. It can be trying, emotional, and frankly overwhelming for most people. However, the last thing a home seller should do is wait until right before the auction to take serious action. At that point, the options are fewer, and thus it may be too late.

The lender will most likely exercise its right to redeem the property, through the foreclosure auction process if necessary. Once the bidding starts at the auction, it is too late. More times than not, the lender itself ends up bidding for its own mortgage and buying the property. At the closing, all liens falling after the foreclosed lien are wiped out. But keep in mind the inverse is also true. There may be liens, ahead of the foreclosing lien, that are not wiped out. For example, there may be another mortgage ahead of the mortgage foreclosing, or property taxes may also be past due. This is the most common event that catches auction investors off guard. Another consideration is that, if there are bidders who pay more than the lien balances due against the property, only some proceeds may go back to the seller.

What are the situations that lead to foreclosures?

The 5% Marketing Solution

In my investing career, I found many commonalities that cause foreclosures to come about. The bottom line is, the parties can no longer afford the payments. In fact it, is common for about **5 percent of all mortgages in this country to fall 30 days late EACH month.** For every one million homes, that means 50,000 people EACH MONTH who fall behind on their mortgage payments. These people are experiencing some distress, you might expect. A person in this situation may not yet be a true "foreclosure deal," but may be just as ready to deal. If you become good at marketing, you can attract many of these people prior to their getting on the public foreclosure lists. This is where a REAL opportunity exists, both to help the homeowner out with more options, and for you to have more buying options with little competition!

Once they do get on public foreclosure lists, you might have a bit more competition, but the seller may also have a lot more motivation. Either way, I'm looking for a way to help these people out, while also finding a profitable deal for myself. I always want a true win-win strategy.

The top reasons people fall into foreclosure:

- Divorce.
- Job loss.
- Excessive debt due to credit cards, auto loans, or excessive refinancing.
- Business failure (four out of five businesses fail within the first five years).
- The wrong kind of mortgage: certain adjustable-rate mortgages might catch up to you.
- Health problems leading to inability to work and/or causing excessive health care payments.
- Robbing Peter to pay Paul. Refinancing debt with debt becomes commonplace, with only one conclusion possible.

As a result of these everyday events, more and more properties fall into default and subsequently become bank-owned properties (REOs - real estate owned).

By the way, even though the housing market is undergoing tremendous growth, the trend is up and not down, for these very reasons.

Here is my basic market position. I believe the place to find flexible and creative deals are prior to the auction of the property. On the other hand, banks end up with properties (REOs), which can also be excellent values to purchase, if the banks are willing to be flexible.

CHAPTER 2
The Mindset and Process of Foreclosure

To a novice, I understand that this discussion about the process of foreclosure may seem a little cold hearted, when you observe it strictly from the perspective of the homeowner in distress.

Please understand that you should approach this business as a professional. You are, in fact, someone who can solve some of the distressed homeowner's problems. You are no guiltier than a psychiatrist whose patient has mental problems, nor than an attorney whose client is a criminal. Foreclosures are just facts of life and always will be a part of the housing industry. It happens with or without you.

Foreclosures have happened in the past, and they will continue to happen, no matter what. You never have to feel like a "home robber" by being in the foreclosure business. You are truly a problem solver. The methods we teach actually make you the "knight in shining armor," whose actions can give people hope for a brighter future. Most importantly, be honest and straightforward with these people. They really need someone like this in their lives. Show them how to make things better.

You might be asking, "Why would any lender make loans to borrowers with little or no money down? Aren't the banks at great risk when they do that?" You might also say, "But they get the property if you don't pay." Believe it or not, this is not always a great deal for the bank. Banks are not in the property ownership and resale business, nor do they want to be. They are only in this business by default.

Understanding Mortgages and the Mortgage Market

There are various types of lenders out there. In the conventional lending market, there are the Federal National Mortgage Administration (FNMA) and the Federal Home Loan Mortgage Corporation. These publicly offered institutions effectively underwrite what we call conventional loans. As an individual, you can invest in their security instruments. This is where they get much of the money to make the loans. Some mortgage brokers would call these "vanilla loans." These types of loans are for excellent credit borrowers with a decent down payment. When you hear of premium rates being offered in the mortgage market, they are usually referring to FNMA loans.

The mortgage market and industry is essentially about risk and return. The higher the risk a lender is willing to take, the greater the return they want on the money. In actuality, it is their investors who put up the money to lend and then demand these criteria to be enforced.

For example, if you're putting very little money down, you might receive or be charged a higher rate. If you're self-employed, you may also receive a higher rate. If your credit is less than perfect (or just plain bad), you may receive a higher rate and be given a lower "loan to value" (loan as a percentage of the value of property). The banks understand how to hedge their risk with lower loan to values and higher rates, in order to offset the effects of foreclosures, which occasionally occur.

If a lender is willing to take on higher risk situations, it is more likely to end up with foreclosures on its books. Frankly speaking, many of what we call higher risk or "nonconforming" lenders expect to end up with some properties in their REO department. Since these lenders usually require a greater down payment, they are better secured by equity. Therefore, they have reduced their risk of loss in the event they have to foreclose and re-sell the property.

Here is another way to look at it. The banks make their money on the "spread of money" which they borrow. Banks really don't lend "their" money. They borrow other people's money and lend it out at a higher rate. The popular term for this is "OPM" or Other People's Money. Many of the greatest riches in the world have been made using OPM. When we buy and sell property, we always try to maximize its use by using OPM vs. our own money, because we actually get a higher rate of return.

For example, say you put $100,000 down to buy a $100,000 property, it appreciates 10% over the next year, and you then sell the property. Your rate of return is 10%.

However, say you put 10% down on the same property ($10,000), it appreciates 10%, and you then sell the property for $110,000. You actually get back your $10,000 down payment PLUS a $10,000 profit on "your money." Remember, $90,000 was OPM. Your rate of return is literally 100% by using the "leverage" of OPM, with even less risk.

"Leverage" is how fortunes are made!

In a hypothetical example for banks, it works like this.

Assume you make a deposit into their account, and they pay you 2%-4% interest on that money. You have "loaned" this money to the bank. The bank then turns around and loans the money out at 6% to 9% on consumer loans. Since they're lending none of their "own money," the spread they earned is virtually pure profit.

In other words they're earning 3% to 7% spread on every dollar in their system. They are really "making" money. If they process $1 million through this system in a day, they may be earning $40,000 to $70,000 for every million dollars they process. Now you know why banks are so willing to lend you money so aggressively. They make even more money as your payments float through, and these can even be loaned again before the banks ever make another loan payment to the ultimate investor. I think of this as the stacking effect. They're making money on top of money making money. You may be thinking, "Maybe I should be in the banking business instead." With real estate, and the proper approach, you can virtually do just that.

Actually, the banks borrow their money from institutions like FNMA, the Federal Reserve Bank, or other private markets which have more money available. It's no wonder they're pushing so hard to get people to borrow, even if certain risks exist. The banks build in the risk factor, anyway, in the form of equity and interest spreads. Banks can't lose, unless they are simply foolish. But consumers can lose, if they're not wise to the system.

The Stages of a Foreclosure

The foreclosure process falls into a few simple stages, which are helpful to understand as an investor.

Stage 1: The Homeowner is Facing Financial Distress.

Perhaps this is due to a job loss, health problem, or they are simply over-financed. Frankly, this is my favorite stage to locate distressed sellers and help them out. This is before their credit has been seriously harmed, and they are not too many payments behind. In many cases, they are not behind at all, at this stage. They are just barely making it.

It is far easier to purchase property at this stage, and I will probably have to come up with less money to make the back payments. This approach assumes you understand how to take over a loan without "assuming" the actual liability for it, by performing a "subject-to" transaction. I have frequently gotten sellers to simply deed the property to me, if I will agree to take over the payments. If they are motivated enough, they will do this.

Stage 2: The Homeowner is Falling Multiple Payments Behind.

At this stage, the homeowners are receiving notices that they are delinquent. They may have begun to receive phone calls from the bank regarding the matter. This is a very uncomfortable stage, as these phone calls are very painful for homeowners to deal with.

They may also be receiving calls from other collection accounts that are falling behind at the same time. This can create a very emotional state for the homeowner. Again, this is an excellent opportunity for you, the investor, to help these people out. If you have the skill to simply have them deed you the property while you agree to make up the back payments, you become the hero. You've just rescued their credit from getting much worse and given them a quick solution to their bleeding payments and credit problems.

Stage 3: Notice of Default

When the dreaded "N.O.D." or notice of default arrives, this is essentially a final warning prior to foreclosure proceedings. In mortgage states, the homeowner can actually receive a summons notifying them of the bank's legal action pending or "lis pendins."

At this point, your credit and this situation are a matter of public record. Just about anyone who goes down to the courthouse can look up these actions. Many investors do go to the courthouse to get this information and begin contacting homeowners at this point. If you're a serious investor, you can learn how to get this information without driving downtown every week.

This can be obtained through a foreclosure service found at my web site: www.tjmarrs.com. Look under the Tools tab.

Additionally, the credit bureaus see the notice of default as a very serious matter on the homeowner's credit. The only thing worse would be an actual foreclosure sale, which is what we want to help these homeowners avoid.

Stage 4:   Notice of Trustee Sale

The "N.T.S." or notice of trustee sale (or something similar in various counties) is the formal notice that indicates an actual auction date is being set.

At this point, the homeowners understand that the clock is truly ticking toward the sale of their house at the courthouse steps. Additionally, there are now multiple back payments due, plus penalties and legal fees, making it even more difficult for the homeowners to cure the problem.

As investors, it is at this stage when we begin to hear from these people. They are now realizing they must act, and act soon. They are even more motivated to act now. I find it quite amazing how many homeowners actually put off things until it gets to this point. In fact, most homeowners wait until just before the auction to start calling investors for help in dealing with the problem. What is important for the investor to understand is this: You must be in position with your marketing, so that these homeowners call you first.

Stage 5:   The Foreclosure Sale or Auction

At the date, location, and time of the notice of trustee sale, an auction will occur that requires the sale of the property to the highest bidder. The bank foreclosing will usually state the minimum bid at which the sale will begin. If the minimum bid is not taken, the bank will purchase back the property, and then it becomes their real estate home or R.E.O.

A note about auctions:

In most cases, the trustee or attorney holding the sale will have payment and bidding requirements. In order to play the game at the courthouse steps, you must show proof of minimum funds and be prepared to place those funds immediately in the trustee's hand.

The strategy I have used involves the use of a cashier's check for the minimum bid, plus a few $5,000 cashier's checks, and a few $1,000 cashier's checks, up to the amount that I am willing to bid. If you don't come prepared, you can't play.

Another note of caution: If you're not fully aware of other liens and encumbrances against the property, or any structural or major repairs it might require, you could be getting into a high-risk situation at the auction.

Know your property before buying. The good news is that if you're buying out a first mortgage lender's position, you should be receiving a relatively clean title, excluding whatever property taxes are due. However, junior liens could be the actual position being auctioned, and there may be more senior underlying liens to be paid. This can get quite complex. The bottom line is, check with your title company and know exactly what you're buying.

Another unique thing that can happen at an auction is that the property may not end up getting auctioned that day, although it was previously scheduled. Sometimes lenders are lenient and give the homeowner more time after some payments or significant negotiations are made. On the other hand, I have had agreements to stop an auction, go to the courthouse steps for some other purpose, only to witness the property I was about to purchase being auctioned off.

This is due to one hand not knowing what the other hand is doing at the bank. Sometimes, they have simply disregarded my purchase agreement with the seller and decided they just want to auction off some other bad debts, regardless of their discussions with buyers like myself.

Auctions can be a fun and exciting time. But auctions offer no flexible terms like the ones you might find when dealing with the seller prior to the auction.

Stage 6: Real Estate Owned (R.E.O.) or Bank Owned Properties

Many investors do quite well by just making offers on these properties.

As banks take back large numbers of properties, they may be willing to significantly discount these properties, so they can get them sold quickly and minimize their losses. Depending on market conditions in the specific area, there may be bargains to be had. Then again, there may not. I've seen situations were banks are very willing to discount, and others where banks are more interested in fixing the properties, and selling them at full retail price. This is a bank-by-bank, market-by-market variable to consider.

Stick to your buying criteria.

Don't get too excited about a foreclosure property, whether it is prior to foreclosure, at the auction, or bank owned. None of this automatically means it will be a "pennies on the dollar" deal. All it means is that you might be dealing with a motivated party that is willing to sell at a significant discount. This is your window to at least try.

CHAPTER 3
Dealing with Homeowners Prior to Auction Pre-Foreclosures

In today's real estate investor environment, many investors are being trained to send a series of letters to these homes, using excellent quality foreclosure lists like those available at www.tjmarrs.com (Tools link). This is an excellent way to streamline your marketing and save time. Of course, you're not the only one who might be sending letters, so having a strong marketing system is also essential.

One option might be to call these homeowners and tell them you can produce cash quickly to help them in their situation. Others may simply choose to go door knocking, which in my opinion is the most effective, but also difficult for many investors to do.

Obviously, these houses are spread around the community, in neighborhoods you may not care to drive through. You also may be nervous about dealing with people who are in such distress. Many will be rude, and some will be nice. That is just part of the business. The bottom line is that if you develop a solid, confident approach and follow-up to develop credibility, you will be better positioned to profit.

Generally speaking, the approach to use when knocking at the door is to indicate you're not there necessarily to buy and sell homes, but that you're there to produce cash for their needs. Let's face it; the problem is not the home. The problem is their financial need for cash. Keep the conversation focused on the subject of their needs. The house is not the problem: Cash to make payments is.

The strategy I like to use in dealing with these homeowners is a **three-step follow-up system**. I've come to understand that these people usually don't jump right on my offer to sell their property, particularly if they have substantial equity involved. On the other hand, I don't want to leave the deal on the table for another investor to come behind me and get a contract that I should have gotten. If you can, get an agreement right away. Leave a clause or two in there that gives the sellers some wiggle room, so they feel they are not over-committing themselves.

One might actually use an option agreement, versus a purchase and sale agreement (more on this in advanced training). The bottom line is to show them that you're flexible and asking them to be equally as flexible.

Another important step, which I show the seller when I first meet with them, is the definition of "net equity." Net equity is what is **left over** after closing costs and payoff of all liens and encumbrances. It is **not** the difference between the price they are offered for their house and their loan payoff.

Very few sellers actually look at this prior to accepting an offer to sell. I am very careful to show them these numbers, being sure that I deduct realtor fees, closing costs, repairs required prior to closing, holding costs, penalties, etc. Why do I do this? To show them they have less equity than they realize. This way, my lower offer won't seem so low. I ultimately insert this phrase, "If my offer is so low, how much will you get if the bank takes your home at the auction?"

I'm not trying to twist anyone's arm here. I am simply showing them the real numbers that they're facing, so they can make a sound decision. Of course, my intent is to get a reduced price; that's just business. I would not be in business long if I paid full price for every house that I bought (or any house that I purchase).

I may also be interested in a strategy where I simply have the seller deed the property to me (giving me full ownership), yet leave the existing loan in place. My intent would be either to get a discount from the current lender, commonly referred to as a short sale. Then I simply bring the payments current and keep the existing loan in place (assuming the terms are good enough to keep in place for a while). This is called a subject-to transaction. This saves me a tremendous amount of money in closing costs and fees, thus securing my increased profit potential.

How to Stop the Foreclosure with Cash

There are many ways to come out with the money to bring the current loan into good standing.

- Use my own cash

- Use my credit to borrow some money

- Use other people's money and create a second mortgage just to ensure their position.

What can you really offer these homeowners?

1. You can buy the house for cash or terms as previously discussed

2. You could guarantee a small loan to make up the back payments and penalties for a guarantee fee (As this is an advanced subject, you want to avoid being construed as an unlicensed lender by not doing this correctly).

3. You could lease the property back to the sellers, until they can refinance and cash you out in exchange for a portion of the equity.

Look for details in our "Home Saver" course.

You might be thinking, "Wait a minute. Why would I make a loan, guarantee a loan, or lease the property to someone who has been in foreclosure?"

This is an obvious question worthy of discussion.

First of all, many people get into foreclosure due to unforeseen circumstances. In many cases the event that caused them to go into default has passed, but it has left them so far behind that they cannot make it up. They may have experienced a lost a job, for example, but now have regained employment. Still, they are so far behind they cannot stop the foreclosure.

If they had significant equity, you could have them deed you the property, which means you, the investor, now own it. You then create a lease agreement with the option to buy, for this party. Be very careful in the processes and procedures you use to separate the agreements. Once the party is in position to get their own financing, they cash you out at the agreed-upon price.

We go into extensive detail on this subject in our advanced workshops. We're seeing investors completely outpace their local investor market with this one strategy alone. **On average, we're seeing investors obtain profits of $20,000 to $80,000 each. Some are doing this several times a month.**

Some of your cash can actually be received on the front end of the transaction, before the buyer even re-purchases the property from you, by using some advanced creative financing. Another advantage is, unlike other rental properties, you usually don't have to worry about finding the tenants, vacancies, dealing with repairs and maintenance, or negative monthly payments. This is all covered for you!

A Simplified Example of a Lease Back Arrangement Using Our Home Saver Plan

(see details in our Bonuses section later)

Current value of the house	$200,000
Current mortgages balance	$150,000
Current payments (PITI)	$1,100
Current arrears	$8,000
	————
Your total cost basis is	**$158,000**

At this point you are given a Warrantee Deed (or equivalent acceptable deed) to the property. You now own the property, even with the existing loans being left in place.

Don't worry about the "due on sale clause." It is really a minimal issue. Odds are, the lender will be happy to avoid the foreclosure. You then simply write a check to cover the $8,000 in arrears to stop the foreclosure. Don't have the $8000? We can show you how to raise that quickly, no problem.

Now, you agree to split any equity with the seller, in some agreeable fashion. The current equity is the difference between your "cost basis," including fees and refinancing costs, and the current market value.

You could also use the future value as the basis, if you so agree.

If your basis is in fact $158,000, you then split the remaining equity from $200,000 current value.

Current or future value of the house	$200,000
Cost Basis(-)	$158,000
(includes your $8,000 invested)	
Total equity to split	$ 42,000
Divided by 2	$ 21,000

Add $21,000 to your original basis in the property of $158,000 = $179,000

This is the re-purchase price for the buyer. This is an equity split.

You then receive back your original $8,000, PLUS a $21,000 profit in 1-2 years! Plus cash flow along the way.

You can either keep the current loan in place, or do a refinance of the current loan. If the latter, you can possibly pull out your share of the profits, in part or in full. The occupant will be making the payments, anyway, and it is quite possible their payments may actually go down as result of the refinance, which helps them out even further. Naturally, you should also keep the profits spread above your payment, in terms of what you charge for the lease.

For example, you might charge $200 above whatever the underlying payment is, in exchange for this arrangement. Over two years, that would be an additional $4,800 returned on your investment.

Using some refinance strategies, processing fees, or cash-out strategies, you can perform this type of transaction in multiple ways.

In either case, you actually help the sellers keep most of their equity, including their future equity, and you still get into the transaction with enough equity to create a secure position for yourself.

Two Common Concerns with the "Home Saver" Approach

1. What if this lease-back occupant person does not perform?

Once they sign the new lease agreement, they are tenants on the property. Most likely, you would evict them, as you would any other tenants not paying their rent. If they have to move on, I would prefer that you work something out about giving them some money for their equity, to end the transaction in an amicable fashion. I don't give away the bank, but I will be fair to try to help these people move on. Remember, you took on a significant risk for them. You already gave them a second chance. You should feel good about that.

2. Is this legal in your state?

This may vary from state to state, and in the process you use to execute this idea. Consult a local attorney on this matter.

CHAPTER 4
Creative Financing Strategies with Foreclosures

There are a multitude of ways to purchase real estate, whether it is a pre-foreclosure or not, without applying for a bank loan. Keep in mind, it does not matter that it is foreclosure property. What matters is the situation and what the sellers need. This is the basis of creative offers.

Sure, you can run down to the bank, pull out a down payment, get a conventional loan, pay thousands of closing costs and hidden fees, and pay full price for real estate. Plus take on all that risk. If that is what you have in mind, you are a speculator. Overpaying for something rarely results in success. Many investors are, in fact, taught to go out and borrow money to buy real estate. I am not a speculator. Borrowing is only a last resort. This forces me to become more creative.

If I buy property at a total cost (including repairs, holding and reselling costs, plus loan cost) that I can't sell today for a decent profit, then I paid too much.

That is my simple formula for success. There are no deals so good that you have to overpay for them. Be patient. Opportunities for good deals exist in every market, if you are constantly in the game looking for them.

Getting the Deed, Subject to Existing Financing

This is the most common way I use to take ownership of foreclosure property. It gives me full ownership, and I actually have a loan on the property, which I might be able to utilize long term. Why would I get a loan in my name, if I don't have to?

The only variable is, where to get the money to bring the back payments current, and cure any other liens against the property. This is where it gets interesting and fun.

Before I ever pay off those back payments, I'm going to approach any secondary lien holders – such as private judgments, second mortgage holders, or others – and ask for a discounted payoff. This is referred to as a "short sale." We have entire advanced courses on just this process alone.

It is not uncommon to get as much as a 90% reduction on some secondary liens. We have seen second mortgages of $50,000 or more reduced to less than $5,000 as a payoff. Why would the lenders accept this? They may get nothing, if the first mortgage holder forecloses. Something is better than nothing.

But what about the dreaded "due on sale clause"

Whenever a student asks me this question, I patiently avoid climbing the wall with the aggravation of having to answer this again. So many people are worried about the dreaded due on sale clause. The due on sale clause, in simple terms, is a paragraph that is found in most mortgages or trust deeds which refers to the transfer of ownership, without paying off the existing loan. It gives the lender "the right" to call the note payable and due, if the title is transferred without the bank's permission. It is a right or a rule, not a law.

I'm not suggesting that you do not notify the lender in some fashion about the transfer of the property to you in one of these situations. In fact, we do let them know: it is just carefully stated. Frankly, the lender is happy to have someone bringing the loan current and make payments. Remember, banks are not in the real estate business, and they do not want to own these properties. In fact, it hurts **their** credit rating to have foreclosures on their record. Their cost of funds and credit also goes up. Therefore, their profit margin and volume goes down.

Many students ask, "What if interest rates go way up? Won't the banks then start calling these loans due?"

Only if they know about it, and if they want to spend the money to go back through every loan in their portfolio, pay $200 each for titles reports (this would cost them millions of dollars), all regarding perfectly performing loans.

It makes no sense. Furthermore, if your bank called your loan due, putting you in a crisis, would you go back to that same bank to get the replacement loan? Of course not. Many investors assume the bank would be stupid enough to expect you to refinance with them, if they called the loan due.

All the bank would be accomplishing is a loss on performing business. Just because interest rates rise does not mean they're losing money, nor will they earn more if they call loans due. If the note is performing, they're making their same spread and fees.

A friend of mine who is an attorney once said, "There is no such thing as due on sale jail." It is not a violation of law to transfer title without paying off a loan. It's that simple. It is nothing more than a contractual right, not an obligation.

When we take titles to properties subject to existing financing, we either take them into the name of our company, or sometimes into the trust (but only to keep the property owner name private). In previous years, we used a land trust for the seller to put title into. This mechanism reduced exposure to the due on sale clause. After a period of years, we have found this is simply too cumbersome and not necessary. Banks simply don't call these notes due, if the payments are current. Of course, they could if they wanted to, because the due on sale clause gives them right to do so. But they don't seem to want to.

Additionally, we have found that title companies prefer a simpler process for tracking title history. Trusts tend to cloud that history in an unfavorable fashion for the title companies. If you can't get title insurance, you can't resell. Our new advanced title holding system takes care of this, without the risks of the trust. I do still use trusts if I already own property and want to have the title held more privately. Using trusts this way creates less exposure to my overall business. Privacy is a form of asset protection.

More Creative Ways to Structure the Foreclosure Purchase

Here is a quick summary of the ways that we have purchased foreclosure properties.

1. Get a new loan and pay cash to pay off the seller (my last choice every time).

2. Take the deed subject to existing financing. Then bring the back payments current, leaving the existing loan in place for a specified period of time. The question then remains, where to

come up with the money?

3. You might use your own cash.

4. Use a partner to put up the cash and split the deal.

5. Use a partner to put up the cash and give them a private party second mortgage, where the issuer is to pay off any existing back payments and mortgages or liens with this new second mortgage. The issuer is to get enough money for repairs as well.

6. Use credit cards or credit lines to bring the back payments current.

Understanding more about the seller's mindset when facing foreclosure

I cannot move forward without discussing this subject for a moment. The sellers are having financial and emotional difficulties as a result of their situation. Please treat these people with respect and understanding, while maintaining your businesslike demeanor and intent.

Too many investors get caught up in these situations and forget that they are there for a reason. Yes, you are driven by profit. The day "profit motive" becomes a bad word is the day our democracy and the free enterprise system are finished. You really can make a situation better, even if it means the homeowner has to move on. Avoiding foreclosure on their credit, as well as the subsequent humiliation it can create, is a gift you can provide them for years to follow.

Patience is a Virtue

Be patient with these people: they will rarely move as quickly as you like. Just make sure they understand that if they don't act quickly, your options to help them become fewer and fewer. Think about it. If the best scenario you can offer is that you go and get a new loan and close, it will take longer than simply writing a check, bringing the payments current (after getting the deed, of course), and perhaps giving the sellers some "walking cash" or a promissory note for part of their equity.

When negotiating, keep asking questions like the ones below. You may have to convince these people that if they procrastinate, it may become too late to help. Those of us who have bought many foreclosure properties know that denial is a common state of mind we deal with, when dealing with foreclosure sellers.

Questions you may ask to convince sellers to move forward:

- What will it feel like to have this taken care of?

- How will you feel if you are treated like a "credit criminal" the next 10 years of your life? (I actually hold out my hands as if they're handcuffed when I say this.)

- Bankruptcy is actually less impacting on your credit than a foreclosure: did you know that?

- How much cash will you get if the house goes to auction? Then you must act now.

Let's examine the reasons the foreclosure business is so good.

It offers large potential profit margins.

EXAMPLE: Anytime you can purchase a commodity below current market value, it is a smart move to take. Even if you have to borrow money to get it, the cost of those funds will usually be far less than the profit you will earn. This is one time that credit is a great thing to have (or the money and credit of others).

Assume you find a $200,000 valued house (fair market value based on other properties in good condition, sold recently in the area, etc.), and there are $170,000 in mortgages against the property, including back payments and penalties.

On the surface, it appears you have $30,000 in equity. In our advanced training, we will show you how to create even more equity with the same deal. You can learn how to double the equity and profit with the right cash flows strategies.

The sellers could end up with ZERO equity in the event of a foreclosure. If they sell through the traditional means of hiring a Realtor, paying traditional closing costs, plus holding costs and a discount for selling quickly, they would likely receive little or no money, anyway.

At least our option is quick and simple. Mostly, it reduces the chances of a foreclosure on their record.

Both parties win:

• The sellers get to save their credit and move on with your help.

- **You get a property at a discount** that you can now resell for a handsome profit. Let's assume you obtained a new loan with a small down payment to purchase the property at $170,000.

  You could sell the property for cash at market value and earn $30,000 **cash now**, minus fees and expenses. Or you could sell on a lease option or an installment land contract for even more profit. If the market is a strong market, you might even sell the property for as much as $220,000 on a contract, plus you might earn a nice monthly cash flow spread.

- **Earn more with creative selling strategies.** Say you have a $50,000 spread + a monthly cash flow of $300 a month (the difference between your mortgage payment and the income from your installment land contract payments from a new buyer). If you hold this for 10 years (120 payments), this equals $36,000 of additional profit. That's a total profit of $86,000 on a property that originally appeared to have less than $30,000 of equity.

- When selling on an installment land contract, **your cash flow is usually in net figures**, as the owner-occupant pays the taxes, insurance, and maintenance. No tenants or toilets required on this method.

- **Both parties also get a faster closing.** Depending on how you purchased the property, your funding source, and methods used, you should be able to close very quickly. At the very least, you should align your strategies so that you can close quickly.

- **Easy financing.** There are many ways you could use to purchase such a property. My favorite would simply be to bring the back payments current, thus stopping the foreclosure, and then start making the existing loan payment. Of course, you get the deed. That is, have the seller transfer title to you, leaving the existing loans against the property. The bank, the seller, and you benefit with this simple arrangement. With this method, you may never need to get a new loan. If you do get a loan, please realize you're taking on more risk. Be careful when you choose to get a loan, especially if you do not have to.

It is a great way to help sellers solve their financial problems and move on with life.

The sellers are facing significant emotional and financial stress. You really can help and need to keep a confident "consulting" mindset. Keep your focus on what these sellers truly need. Selling the house just solves part of the problem: it's not the entire solution.

More Creative Ways to Purchase a Property
Purchase using a "Lease Option."

This is nothing more than an agreement to lease the property, and have established a purchase price built into what we call an "option agreement." When purchasing, I would typically use a single form, combined lease option document. I must strongly caution you here, though, that you are relying on a person in financial distress to follow through later with a promise of delivering title. You must take certain provisions to have the title previously signed and held in escrow, pending your completion of the contract, at which time you would then received the deed. This is only a rare backup strategy that you should use only if the seller won't deed you the property at the beginning.

Purchase by getting a deed "subject to" existing loans.

This is simply a process where the seller signs a warranty deed or similar instruments to transfer title to you, while leaving the existing loans against the property. But in the end, I would much rather have the deed early and quickly with these sellers who tend to be a little unreliable. If I have the deed, I own the property, regardless if the previous liens are against it. Of course, a foreclosure could still happen, which would simply mean I don't get to keep the property, but it is not on my credit record when this happens.

Purchase outright with cash or new financing.

As long as there is significant equity, this is a great strategy to use. Just be sure to work with a lender who can reliably close before the auction date, or your efforts will be for naught.

You may also end up using a combination of these strategies, depending on the seller's mood, or various other circumstances. Be ready, and be flexible.

We strongly suggest you have a basic understanding of these creative financing methods before venturing into foreclosures. The purpose of our Advanced Training program is to help you apply that knowledge to the field of pre-foreclosure investing.

CHAPTER 5
Build Your Pre-Foreclosure Business Like a "Real" Business
STEP-BY-STEP

1. Locate prospects.

Check our glossary for ways to can get your hands on weekly leads. Then, start the process of writing letters or cards. Note that some of these sources also provide this service for you. Anytime you can save some time, money, or effort, take advantage of it. You'll find this is a numbers game that requires you to automate much of the process, in order to compete. Don't be "penny wise and pound poor."

2. Evaluate transactions carefully and perform due diligence.

You need to be able to evaluate a transaction quickly to determine its viability. Time is of the essence when dealing with pre-foreclosures.

3. Construct transactions as we have taught

Quick reminder, there are 3 Ways to Profit in the Foreclosure Buying Business

    a. **Buy, then quickly sell.**

        Obviously, when you sell the property, you are going to cash out the old loan, thereby stopping the foreclosure. This equates to quick cash.

    b. **Buy and hold the property using the current loans.**

        This means you need to have the ability to take ownership of the property. Get the deed signed over to you and get the loan reinstated quickly with available funds or loans. We often refer to this process as taking the property "subject to" existing financing or a "subject to" transaction. This method may require you to put some money into the transaction to make it all work. If you buy at low enough prices, it is fairly safe to use your own credit to bring the back payments current, negotiate a reduced payoff with the lender, make necessary repairs, and hold the property until you resell.

        When you find buyers, their down payment can go into your pocket or to pay off the initial money you borrowed.

    c. **Buy the property with a new mortgage.**

        There are more risks with this method, but you also buy more properties as a result of having this option available.

        You could use a partner with down payment and credit to buy these, if you don't have sufficient credit yourself.

This last type of money can be expensive, but if your margins are large enough, it works. It is better to pay a higher rate to borrow money and earn $30,000 than to seek a lower rate and not earn anything from your efforts.

Take the money, *please*!

Then it becomes time to exercise an effective "exit strategy." Your strategy will be determined by your immediate needs, be they short-term cash or long-term wealth building.

Essential Skills You Should Develop

...in addition to learning more about real estate:

Learn to negotiate effectively:

Study as many books as you can on the art of negotiation. I can tell you from my own experiences, you will develop your own style. But there are certain things that work in this business better than others. The bottom line is, don't be afraid to negotiate. I consider negotiating to be where my money is made. It's where I beat the competition. So if competition is an issue with you, learn to negotiate better. I LOVE to teach Power Negotiating: it is truly the million-dollar skill and is very teachable.

Get a thorough understanding of the foreclosure process in your region or state.

If you know a local attorney who can explain the foreclosure process in alive environment, buy lunch and learn about how foreclosure works in your area. Quite frequently, there are many local issues you need to be aware of, which a real estate attorney can help you better understand. If you know a real estate broker who is also well versed in foreclosures, ask for a personal consultation. Realtors eat lunch, too.

Built a "dream team" of professional associates

You'll find executing this business alone to be somewhat difficult. But if you have a good realtor, a good lender, title company, attorney, contractor, accountant, and other key people, you will accelerate the process and make your life easier.

Set up a professional office

At first, a simple home office will do. Try to established a place where you can keep your work separate from your home life. Remember, this is a business. If it looks and feels like one, it will more likely become one.

You might consider a professional mentor or coach, or seek advanced training from the best experts you can find.

This is where we feel we can help you the most. Be sure to check out our resources for additional training, found at www.tjmarrs.com .

How to select a good Realtor and why

First of all, a good Realtor can be a great source of foreclosure leads to you. They can bring pre-foreclosure deals, as well as those already owned by the bank. If you want their attention, however, be sure you can perform on your side of the deal. Interview these Realtors carefully, to be sure they understand what your buying criteria are, and be sure they bring you only those deals. It is far too easy for them to bring the wrong deals, which only increases your risk of loss.

Realtors can also be a good resource for other services and resources you might need along the way. For example, you might need a referral to the lender, a title company, attorney, or other professionals essential to your success.

Short Sales and Working with Realtors

This is what I do...

Would you like to take possession of properties with existing loans against them, and then simply ask the lenders to reduce the payoff balances on those loans, thus creating more equity for you? Of course you would.

Unless you were just sleeping when you read the last sentence, you are learning about a huge profit center.

Many times, in these foreclosure situations prior to the auction, lenders will discount their payoffs in order to cut their losses. This is a very carefully thought-out process. It combines some skill, negotiation, recognition of the right deals to attempt, and time. We do offer more advanced training on this subject in our courses. I will give you this advice, however. Find a Realtor who likes to negotiate short sales for other people, and they will do most of the work for you. Of course, be sure they are actually experienced and skilled at this, or they may just get in your way, rather than help. They usually negotiate their fee right into your payoff with the bank.

CHAPTER 6
REOs, Bank Owned Property Secrets

Why do banks get stuck with real estate owned, or REO properties?

Simply put, banks get stuck with properties when they don't have enough equity in the property to get it sold to an investor prior to an auction. If there is little equity in the property, there may not be bidders at the auction who are willing to buy the property at a high market price. Therefore, the bank ends up owning the property after that auction.

Also, if the property is in relatively bad condition, it may not draw a sufficient price in order for an investor to purchase it at the auction or prior to that date. Therefore, the bank, once again, ends up with the property. It's always been my considered opinion that the best deals happen prior to the auction and prior to the REO list, but there are exceptions.

Oftentimes, a bank will end up with the property, because it would not negotiate with the investors who wanted to purchase prior to the auction. The bank simply wasn't willing to accept the offer and ends up owning a property that's in poor condition. They may lose even more money on it. These, quite often, are the properties which investors end up purchasing at extremely low prices. By extremely low prices, I'm referring to forty to fifty cents on the dollar. Not bad.

Another situation where the bank might unwittingly end up with the property is when there is an IRS lien, or child support is attached to the property. The IRS could have 120 days to take back the property, even after the auction. Many investors simply don't want these properties because of that risk, so the bank ends up with it. If the bank does end up with this type of property, it wants to get rid of the property quickly. It is rare that the IRS will really do much, if there is little apparent equity.

So why will banks sell properties at low prices?

If banks take back too many properties, it negatively affects their credit rating with the Federal Reserve and with private investors. Additionally, the PMI insurance, which normally protects the bank to some degree, is going to fight paying the insurance to the bank whenever possible. They're going to look for partial settlements versus full settlements to the bank. The bank can still lose. As with any form of insurance, they're going to resist paying.

Banks have to get rid of these properties, before it's too late. If they cause the bank to incur a higher or more negative credit rating, these losses may damage the banks' credit ratings. Like consumers who have bad credit, banks whose ratings are low pay higher interest on the money they borrow to lend. As a result, banks could also end up losing money, because they become less competitive, receive smaller margins, and make fewer loans.

Further, when banks make large numbers of non-performing loans, these banks are going to be more heavily scrutinized by the government. Again, this is something banks would rather avoid, for obvious reasons. These banks typically are labeled as being abusive and taking unnecessary risks with their clients. They don't want that reputation.

Another thing banks consider is that they don't really want to fix up these properties. They want to move them quickly. In some regions, we have seen a recent trend where banks do go ahead and fix up some of the properties. This only occurs in rare instances, where there is significant appreciation going on in that market. In these markets, banks can possibly make up some of their losses by fixing up properties and selling at full retail price.

Finally, banks simply don't want to manage and maintain these properties. In most cases, they'll hire good realtors to go out and market these properties for them, rather than do it themselves. They don't want these properties, and they don't want to deal with it. This is where you, as a smart investor, come in.

So where does the investor fit in? How can you profit?

The bottom line is that these banks will dump these properties, especially if they are in disrepair. In other words, they know these properties won't sell easily "as is," and they don't want to hold on to the property and incur significant holding costs over a long period of time. They will tend to sell these properties based upon the "time cost" of holding properties, rather than their financial investment alone in the property. They simply don't want this property. It's all about the money, and they don't want to lose it.

Would you?

Many of these properties are in a fairly poor condition, for some very obvious reasons. The owner walked away. They may have abused the property. Maybe there were even some serious mental or physical issues involved, which did not allow this person to take good care of the property. Whatever the reason, the banks end up with massive liability on their hands, which needs to be to taken care of soon.

The Trick to Succeeding with REOs

The simplest strategy I can give an investor for finding REOs and getting some of your offers accepted is to make lots of offers. But where do you find these REO properties?

> I strongly recommend you look take the free trial on our web site www.tjmarrs.com (click on the "Tools" link)

There are many REO properties listed there and updated regularly. You can also obtain other important information, such as comparable sales, tax and sale data, and more. You can even find a Realtor, also available through that same site, that can represent you in making offers on these properties. The bottom line is that this is a numbers game, and you have to make a lot of offers to be successful.

Secondly, you need to be prepared to close with immediate financing. Most banks want to close quickly, so have your financing prearranged with your mortgage broker or bank. Move in quickly, pay cash, fix the property, and then you might consider refinancing. Pull back all of your cash out of the property quickly, so that you're into the property with very little of your own money. Remember, OPM – other people's money – is where fortunes are made.

Always have the strategy of getting in there, buying it quickly, and then refinancing out to pull your cash out of the property and move on to the next property. Preserve your capital and lines of credit for the short term moves.

Precautions to Consider in the REO Business

1. Stay away from **poorly located** properties. If a property sits next to a porno shop, or there's drug dealing going on down on the corner, you might want to think twice about owning this property.

2. Be careful of properties that might be in **remote rural areas** that are hard to find or inconvenient for people to live in. Most people want to live in centrally located areas, where they have easy access to convenient services and feel it's basically a nice neighborhood to live in.

3. Also be aware of **hidden physical problems** that properties might have. They could have zoning problems. They could have sewage problems. There could be problems with the water systems that are out there, or problems with the mold in the property, or other such conditions that you need to think of. Beware of very poor condition situations. Also be aware of the high cost of demolition and destruction, or hauling off of materials, as may be necessary.

4. Be very aware of what the property is really worth. My process goes like this: I contact a local title company, and I get information on "actual sales" of similar properties of similar size in that area during the last six months. DO NOT rely on "tax assessed" values. Be sure you personally see every property prior to purchase, and compare it to those comparable properties you also drive by, in person.

Choosing a Good Real Estate Agent for Investor Relationship

In choosing a real estate agent, you need to think very carefully about working with an agent who is positive about the idea of working with investors. I found many agents out there who simply don't want to work with investors, because they've had bad experiences with them.

These bad experiences might include:

1. The investor could not perform, or close as agreed, on anything.

2. The investor and the realtor could not communicate.

3. The investor made way too many offers without closing.

4. The Realtor wasn't willing to do the work. The bottom line is, you do need to make a lot of offers when dealing with REOs, and not all of them will work out. You need a Realtor who will work with you and who will be patient with you. But you have your part to do as well.

Services your agent can help you with

Your agent should also be willing to find things such as:

1. Market data, time on market, and comparable sales values for you.

2. A good Realtor will do a lot of work and earn their wages, and you as   an investor need to be ready to perform, which means have your   money ready and be ready to close when good deals come along.

What should you pay to guarantee profit security? Know your "CTV"

In considering your cost, or what you should pay for a property, I use the term "CTV" –"cost to value." I look at every potential cost of buying, fixing-up, holding, carrying, and reselling the property. I also consider the costs of borrowing and refinancing the property. You should have a general idea of what these things are going to cost, as they will creep up on you and bite into your profit significantly, if you are not prepared.

Cost to value, or CTV, is the maximum percentage that I'm willing to go, in getting involved with a particular deal.

For example, if a property is worth

Fair market value after repairs (FMV/ARV):   **$200,000**
then I might be willing to pay 80% of ARV as my maximum CTV.

In other words I'd be willing to pay 80% CTV: **$160,000**
minus all of the potential costs of the property, and then I come to what my actual price would be that I offer the bank. If my total miscellaneous costs would run $15,000, I would take $160,000 minus (-) $15,000 dollars, and therefore offer $145,000 to the bank as the all-cash net price.

Always work backwards from the final value.

CHAPTER 7
Foreclosure Auctions: Deals are Waiting on the Courthouse Steps

When pre-foreclosure properties meet their fate and go to the auction sale, it is too late for the homeowner who wishes to stop the foreclosure. The property has been foreclosed on, and is either owned by a new purchaser at the auction, or by the foreclosing bank itself, which buys back the property at that time.

In most cases, if the property has substantial equity and goes to the auction sale, it may be purchased at an extremely low price by a wise investor who is aware of the opportunity and prepared for action. The key is to have an understanding of the property's final value, after repairs. Once again, you need to make a careful determination as to the actual cost-to-value ("CTV") that the property may cost you to buy, hold, fix-up, and resell.

Cash is King

In fact, it is the only thing allowed here.

Having this in mind, you can back down from the CTV, into what should be your maximum cash price paid for the property at the auction sale. Cash is King at the auction. In fact, it is the only welcome guest at an auction. If you're going to buy property at auctions, you must have a strategy as to how you're going to pay for it. Most auctioneers require that you bring a large sum of cash, a series of cashier's checks, or at least a cashier's check with the minimum amount of the bid. Be sure to contact the trustee holding the auction to determine their bidding and payment rules.

In any case, you need to be ready to move quickly – with cash. So where can you come up with this money? Certainly, you could go with private party monies, credit lines, cash, or private mortgage investors who issue what we call hard money. There is literally a ton of cash awaiting a good rate of return out there. Watch out for our "Raising Cash Fast Training," elsewhere in this course or online.

Be sure you have your cash all lined up prior to getting to the auction. If the particular auction property you are seeking is vacant, this could be an additional opportunity to get the property cheaply. It could be an opportunity for two reasons. First of all, other pre-foreclosure investors may not have been able to reach these homeowners to negotiate a deal prior to the auction (likely because they did not know how, as we teach you). Another reason is that many investors may have gotten a hold of the sellers, but never got to see the inside, thus they did not act. What may be a risk for others may become your opportunity.

Critical Auction Mistake to Avoid

Be sure that any auction property that you might be bidding on is, in fact, the first mortgage that is foreclosing. First trust deeds and first mortgages are the ones in first lien position against the property (excluding property taxes). If a second trust deeds or mortgage is foreclosing, you could be fooled into purchasing a property for essentially the value of the second trust deed, not realizing there might be underlying IRS liens, property taxes owed, or even a first mortgage, in addition to what you thought you were paying for the property. This is a common mistake people make at auctions, so be sure you work closely with someone on your first auction who understands this process. The simple answer is, get a preliminary title report as part of your final step in making bids.

The insider's strategy to protecting yourself at an auction

This one is very simple. Go with someone who's bought property at an auction before. They're going to be the ones to give you some great insights about what's going on at this auction, at this particular location, and about auction investing in general. A mentor is really the key.

Where to find out where auctions are to be located?

When an action is to be held, a public notice is usually required. Certainly the Public Notices of Trustee Sale, or whatever they're called in your given area, will list this information. Online resources are other good sources of properties that are in pre-foreclosure and soon heading to the auction. Usually, you will find that the local newspaper is also a good resource for auction notices. You can also go to the courthouse for updates and notices. The courthouse should have dates and times of auctions coming up.

Another good resource might be foreclosure trustee or attorneys. These are the people working with the lender to take back the property through the foreclosure process. They put together extensive lists of properties that they're about to foreclose on. Some have web sites full of this information. You may wish to contact them prior to the auction, just to be sure of the terms and conditions that may be offered at the auction. While you're doing that, you can establish a relationship where you get on their notification list for properties that are going to auction.

After you successfully purchase the property as an REO or auction property

The post-closing steps required are similar to buying any property. That is, you need to get insurance, title insurance, new locks, and begin repairs on the property. Consult with our extensive checklists in our advanced courses.

Frankly, auction purchasing is the simplest way to buy a property. It's an all-cash deal; you get a clear title if you do it correctly. You now own the property outright, with a lien granted to your money-lender (if applicable), ready to sell it at a significant profit. Once you clean up the property, you could then refinance it and hold it long term as a rental, sell on a lease option, or perhaps sell it with an installment land contract (see our Creative Financing Course).

Obviously, if you sell it for all cash, you'll receive your cash sooner, but you should also consider the tax implications of selling in less than one year of ownership, vs. holding over one year. The final profit outcome could be significant. Consult you tax advisor on that one.

CONCLUSION

Now, it is up to you to act. If you need to study more, do so. If you need a mentor or coach, let us know. See our Resources directory in the back of the book. Whatever you do, don't make the critical mistake of confusing "study" with productive activity. There is a difference. Too much study can even backfire on you, by creating too many ideas and too great an obstacle to overcome.

What is the number one mistake to avoid?

Letting fear of the unknown stop you. I think of mistakes I might make by taking an action as far less costly than failing to act. How will your future ever change, if you don't change first? You have to be willing to take on a few uncomfortable risks, in order to obtain the wealth and success you what you want? Staying comfortable will ultimately keep you uncomfortable in the future.

See you in the "Success Circle" soon...please join us. All you have to do is choose to be there.

T.J. Marrs
www.tjmarrs.com

SPECIAL BONUS SECTION

T.J.'s Million Dollar "Reverse Foreclosures" Real Estate Investing System

By T.J. Marrs
www.tjmarrs.com

"Reverse Foreclosure Investing"

Helping Homeowners Keep Their Homes Out of Foreclosure, Keep Their Dignity, and Save Their Credit, So Everybody Wins!

So you want to buy cheap foreclosure houses and sell them for a great profit!

Ask yourself one very important question while considering the foreclosure real estate investing business. Why would someone want to sell you their home? While you and your competitors are out there offering to purchase someone's distressed property at a huge discount below what it is worth, so they can leave and give you the equity in the property, you are communicating a message to home sellers which is inverse to their actual desire. It is no wonder that sellers do not respond positively to most of the foreclosure marketing that is produced out there by your competitors.

How would you like to have a way to get three to four times as many of these home sellers calling you first, before the competition, all the while helping the home seller get what they want? Then pay close attention to the following two breakthrough strategies.

Why not deliver a message that tells the homeowners what they really want to hear? The message is NOT "give up your equity." instead, it could be, "You don't have to sell your home. In fact, we will help you keep your home and save your credit."

A properly structured message, combined with a more desirable offer, is more likely to get a positive response from one of these homeowners. One of the great truths of marketing is to deliver a message and product that implies a positive emotional response, not a negative one. Most investors are sending out ads which speak of "getting out of foreclosure" combined with a message which implies "we want to take your equity."

The following two techniques, which I referred to as "Home Saver Plans," not only deliver the message that these homeowners want to hear, but it delivers the desired results as well.

The simple fact is, more times than not, homeowners want to stay in their property. You'll get a higher response rate to your marketing by capitalizing on this desire, and advertising your plan which **may** allow homeowners to remain in their house.

How do you actually make money doing that?

We will get to that shortly.

First, a note of caution:

Be careful how your offer is worded, because it may not apply to many situations. If you want to market and make this kind of offer, use some degree of caution. You may even want to consult with a local attorney about the implications of such advertising or protections to implement based upon local laws. Do not overtly state that you are making loans or offering leasebacks. Simply imply you can stop their foreclosure, help them get the money they need, and help them stay in their home, if they qualify.

When you purchase a property from a homeowner, then turn around and allow the seller to lease the property back from you with an option to buy, you are offering the seller a lease purchase option (LPO). Be sure the seller's financial situation has changed significantly from the original circumstances that caused their payment default.

Another consideration to be aware of, not every person facing foreclosure is a candidate for this strategy. When you first heard of this approach, your first thought might be, "Why would I lease back to someone, or make a loan to someone, who has just gone through such a rough time financially?" Believe it or not, there are criteria you can follow where your money is safe.

For example, if a homeowner was laid-off from work for a period of time and is now back to work, and can prove it (but unable to cure the back payments now), he or she may be a good candidate.

They should also have substantial equity. If they have substantial equity, they are less likely to *sell* to an investor, anyway. It is amazing how many investors run around looking for just these deals, but have the absolute reverse message and product that will get a response from many sellers. So let's change all of that, shall we?

Home Saver Strategy No. 1
The Sale Lease Back, Equity Share Strategy

T he first way I will show you how to profit from this approach involves buying the property, then leasing it back to the original seller. This is also known as an "LPO, Lease Purchase Option."

Here are the steps:

1. You purchase the property. You may either get a new loan to buy the property or you may acquire the property using a "subject to" strategy, by getting the seller to simply give you a deed to the property, while you assume responsibility for making the existing payments. Get details on creative financing in our advanced course on creative financing.

2. You then lease the property back to the seller, assuming you can bring the payments current on the existing loan and wait for your equity later. You would effectively be splitting some of the equity profit at some future date with the original owner after your costs, based upon fair market value then.

To determine your final profit split with the original owner, simply determine an acceptable formula all parties can agree to, and calculate a split between fair market value when they re-purchase, minus your original cost and expenses.

There are several ways in which to structure the transaction to your greatest favor, but let's keep it simple for now. The bottom line is, you own the house with a new or existing mortgage on it. Of course, it might be to your advantage to have good credit and some cash to work with in this situation.

There are a few tips to keep in mind, when using this approach.

1. Check the seller's credit and review their overall history.

Treat them as you would a brand new tenant in terms of paperwork and due diligence. Of course, the credit may not look good, but look for certain *patterns*. You're looking for a candidate who had an unfortunate event recently happen in their lives, which caused them to fall behind, but it now seems they have gotten past that event, and are at least on the road to a recovery. For example, they just started work again after a layoff, but now can't catch up or get a loan to correct the past problem.

Caution: You would likely want the property deeded to you before you bring the payments current, to stop the foreclosure auction while you line up new financing.

2. Stick to solid equity situations only.

Be sure there is a certain amount of equity in the property, to protect you against any problems that might arise with this tenant/buyer. If they do not pay, the property becomes yours, and they are evicted. That may sound rather short and cruel, but it is simply the business of real estate. They must fulfill their end of the deal, and you must fulfill your end of the deal.

You should have AT LEAST 15% to 20% equity in the property, based upon its fair market value MINUS any transaction costs or repairs.

For example: $200,000 FMV property (after repair fair market value). Your new mortgage should not exceed 85% (MAX.) of this amount, or in terms of dollars = $170,000.

This new loan should cover the existing loan payoff, back payments pay off, any other debts or liens, insurance, fees, transaction fees, and of course, some cash in your pocket (which would count against your equity share later).

Be sure to factor in ALL costs of buying and re-selling as part of your costs, when determining how much you should pay for this property. If the loan balances are too high, you probably don't have the deal. There are enough situations out there where the proper equity exists, so you should not have to take on high-risk situations or overpriced properties.

In fact, you should not even have to take on situations that require a short sale (lender discount) to make it work out, in most cases. Short sales are more cumbersome and difficult than lease-back scenarios. Stick to solid equity deals if you can. Deals are plentiful, without the hassle of begging for equity from the banks.

3. The final step is to complete the paperwork for the tenant buyer to repurchase the property from you.

Note: Keep the buying and re-selling paperwork separate. In fact, do the buying and selling paperwork and transaction on different days, to differentiate between the two distinct transactions. It is our experience that failing to make a distinction between transactions could get you into legal hot water, if the arrangement with the seller/tenant does not work out at some point down the road. Your objective is simply to have the homeowner pay you a lease payment, which more than covers your monthly expenses. Ideally, the payments could go down for these homeowners, based upon favorable low payment loans you may be able to establish. Now, that's helping the home seller out even more!

Although you are not automatically doing anything illegal, it only takes a good attorney for the original homeowner, to tie up **your** property in litigation, and frivolously claim their client was not clear on what was happening, or that they signed an agreement under financial or emotional duress.

If you do proceed with a LPO transaction, purchase the property outright first. Get the deed into an "equity holding trust" (refer to our Land Trust Course), then have the seller's interest assigned to you or get a new loan.

Once purchased, enter into a lease agreement, with a *separate* option agreement with the tenant/buyer/original seller. Be very clear with the original seller that these are two distinct transactions.

You absolutely must have some solid disclosures, disclaimers, and a well-written lease agreement based upon experiential real estate investing, and not just legally correct. You may have to negotiate the terms for the purchase in one of several ways. Do whatever works for both parties. But remember to treat the lease purchase option as a brand new transaction with an unfamiliar tenant/buyer.

A possible special clause to add to the option agreement with the buyer:

Buyer price will be a 50/50 split between the appraised value at the time of exercise of option value minus the seller's stated original basis cost of approximately $_____, this may be adjusted upward based on any additional unforeseen seller costs incurred during any lease arrangement with buyer.

The "cost" you will list should include all of your loan costs, fees, loan payoffs, back payments paid, special transaction arrangement fees if we assist you, your pre-paid management fee, legal fees, etc. Account for everything, so you have a basis from which to calculate your equity share later.

You can work out whatever formula you want. We have found this one to be the most equitable. But be careful how it is worded, and be careful of the nature of documents used. You do not want to inadvertently create an "equitable title" problem, thus making it difficult to get this tenant buyer out if you need to.

WITH A SUCCESSFUL "LPO," EVERYONE WINS

- The sellers remain in their original home in exchange for sharing *some* equity.

- You have an instant buyer for a property you just bought. No repairs, marketing or holding time or costs (like other investors have with properties they're trying to sell).

- You are protected as fully deeded owner, until the client exercises their option and actually purchases the property from you. By being careful about the process, you can easily get rid of this tenant, and re-sell quickly if necessary. As a landlord, you can simply evict these tenants if they do not perform, and then resell the property on the open market.

- You could potentially get *cash back* upon *purchasing* the property, rather than waiting until you resell to pull cash out. If you choose to enlist our services as mentor/coach, or as a trustee, we can show you how to do this even better. Normally, lenders do not allow cash back on investment properties. We can show you this amazing strategy to get cash up front in a one-on-one setting only. Don't bother asking your lender for this. Cash-in on our secret, rather than waiting two to four years to receive most of your profit.

Would an extra $20,000 to $30,000 cash in your pocket, upon the *purchase* of each of these, help in your investing venture?

Meanwhile you're helping out these home sellers in a wonderful way that only a properly trained master investor could.

Some scenarios of helping distressed sellers out:

1. Foreclosure Bail-Out.

   a. Property owner first deeds over title to you. You then hold onto the property, and possibly leave their current loan in place, if it is at a favorable rate. You might then refinance, or get a new loan as a purchase – depending on lender requirements. Be sure to make a clean separation from your purchase agreements and any other agreement you make with the seller.

b. Only take on deals with significant equity. Keep in mind that if WE refer you a deal, we also take a commission and profit share position for finding and co-managing the property, under our "Home Saver" Program.

c. Some of the cash taken out of the equity loan is placed in reserve to pay down the mortgage, insurance and taxes - and is held by an attorney in escrow or with and escrow company.

d. A great way to structure the deal is to let the client lease the home from you at a **reduced payment for the first 6-12 months.** You actually pull some cash out of the loan to offset the reduced rent amounts you placed in reserve. Or you could opt to offer to make their first 3 payments FOR them, giving them enough time to get re-established. Of course, factor in any payments made for them, when calculating their re-purchase price.

e. At 6 - 36 months later, the original homeowner buys the property back from you, with a new loan or on private contract terms, using the lease payment history as their alternate credit.

f. You are out, and they have saved their house.

g. After, you could roll them into an installment contract sale. This will better cover any potential loan payment adjustments you may have down the road. You may offer this option, after the second full year of successful payments. But the occupant's payments (and your cash flow) will likely go up. This further helps them establish credit, plus you could increase the payment, to create a nice additional cash flow for you. You may also structure the terms so that the payment adjustments keep up with any underlying mortgage payment increases, using a "mirror" adjustment payment strategy.

You make your cash 3 ways:

1. You may pull some cash out from the original creative purchase. Or get the deed first, then refinance and pull cash out, using a private friendly lien we show you how to place.

2. You will likely earn a monthly cash flow difference between what the client/tenant/buyer pays you, and what the underlying mortgage payments equal.

3. You will then earn the equity share profit upon resale to the client/tenant/buyer. You are cashed out when they re-purchase. There are various formulas to use to calculate this split. I simply take my acquisition costs, after discounts and short sale adjustments, and subtract that from the appraised value when the occupant purchases. I then divide that amount of equity 50/50 with them to determine their final price.

TYPICAL EXAMPLE:
Everybody wins

Current loan balances and liens with penalties	$200,000
The loan payoffs & expenses (=) no more than 85%	$170,000

(This includes my new loan costs, management fees, payments made on their behalf, set up fees, etc.)

When the tenant/buyer repurchases the property	
it apprises for (=)	$240,000
My total costs and fees incurred:(-)	$170,000
(this could include a management fee)	
Equity gain to split (=)	$ 70,000
X 50%(-)	$ 35,000

Occupant Re-Purchase Price Calculation

Value	$240,000
(-) equity share (=) your profit (+) monthly cash flow	$ 35,000
Net re-purchase price to the tenant/buyer	**$205,000**

If I had withdrawn any portion of my equity in the original refinance, I would also factor that into the equity split with the tenant/buyer, as a draw against my share of the equity split. You want to keep it fair and equitable.

A real world example of one associate's results...
What if you only do a small percentage of these numbers?

This is just one investor's activity in his 24 months of using this strategy.

NOTE: This is just one investor's documented activity during the first 30 months using this strategy. It is not a guarantee of results of results, or representative of all students' success.

- Total equity share transactions $40,500,000
- Total investor equity $9,720,000
- Avg purchase price $225,000
- Average equity per gain per deal! $54,000
- Average monthly cash flow $217
- Average LTV (excellent equity) 76%
- Total clients saved 180
- % of reported transactions where occupant has failed to fulfill re-purchase agreement (as of Jan. 2004) <4%

In these cases, you end up with the entire property equity.

Investor Benefits:

- You rarely have to deal with **vacant properties.**
- You will rarely deal with **re-selling hassles,** holding costs, or risks.
- Rarely deal with **repairs and upkeep.**
- Earn **THREE streams of cash flow:** upon purchase, monthly cash flow, and any lump sums due upon re-selling back to the tenant/buyer!
- Get home sellers **calling you first,** and last (with the proper marketing strategy).
- **Retire young and rich,** while helping people out!

The advantages of learning this advanced strategy.

You earn profits from the people who don't ever want to sell to your competitors. You offer them more of what they WANT! They can stay in their homes and get a second chance. Another great advantage when buying these properties is that you rarely have to worry about vacancies or finding buyers. They are already living on the property. The only trick is picking the right situations that have a great likelihood of working out.

You also need a proven and tested marketing strategy. If you are in our private coaching system, and you follow our marketing plan, we guarantee you can do **2 deals in the first 120 days = $40,000 minimum equity profit***.

How does that compare to your current investment plan and strategy, or other offers?

*Certain conditions apply, call today.

Home Strategy #2
Private Secured Financing for Homeowners in Distress

- Give distressed home sellers what they really want.

- Earn $10,000 to $15,000 each time, cash in your pocket.

- Make money on deals with the home seller who would never call an investor to give up their equity.

What do homeowners in foreclosure really WANT, 90% of the time?

Do they want to sell? No. This is precisely why so many real estate investors fail at the foreclosure business. They strictly focus on marketing a message that people do not want to respond to. This is contradictory to the very nature of marketing, or what even makes sense.

Don't get me wrong: Purchasing properties in foreclosure is a wonderful way to get wealthy, or at least make some good money in real estate. However, this only works if you approach that strategy as just one portion of an overall investor strategy.

The easiest thing to do when marketing a product is to deliver a product and a message, which is exactly what the consumer of the product wants. Then making the sale is easy.

But how do you make money doing that?

Is selling the property to you, then leasing it back, the homeowners' first choice, if they have a better option? Not always. It is a great option for some who are properly evaluated, though. We totally believe in the sale-leaseback strategy that we teach. But again, it does not fit every situation, particularly when there is a lot of equity involved.

There are essentially **3 ways in which to make money with pre-foreclosures.** This section will now focus on this **third** strategy.

1. Our advanced foreclosure-investing course and workshops.
2. Our sale-leaseback strategy.
3. The strategy of getting the seller the money they really want (and still making money doing it).

Most sellers simply want one thing: to keep the house and keep the title in their name.

Ask yourself this common sense question: If you had a 30% or more net equity in your property, as a percentage of its value, would you do anything and everything to avoid giving that up to an investor? Of course.

With this basic understanding, we can approach the problem with the third solution for foreclosure-distressed homeowners. Someone facing foreclosure is going to be under a great deal of duress. They will stall, delay, shop around, or anything to avoid selling and giving up their precious equity and home. So why not have a strategy up your sleeve that will help them do just that?

Here is a breakdown of what you can expect in the foreclosure business, depending on the equity in the property.

1. **The homeowner has 20 percent or <u>less</u> equity remaining in the property.**

These folks are most likely to simply give you the deed to their property and walk away. What if they have far less equity than that? You better have some creative strategies up your sleeve, which require very little money or risk, in order to, manage these properties for a significant profit. Our advanced "Cash Flow Explosion" deal making courses and Pre-Foreclosure courses cover this in detail. Go to www.tjmarrs.com.

2. **The homeowner has 20 to 30 percent or greater equity remaining in the property.**

This homeowner is beginning to have enough equity that they're not as likely to respond to investors sending them letters who want to take their equity away. On occasions this situation will work out, but more likely they would be responsive to a lease-back scenario.

3. The homeowner has 30% or more equity in the property, they are less likely to be responsive to an investor solicitation to give up their equity.

Even if you try and hide the underlying message within your marketing, they will smell a rat. Instead, we suggest you offer to help them get the money they want to clear up all of their urgent property financial problems and keep their home. This will serve you far better than trying to force a transaction they don't want. Most importantly you can make a lot of money doing this, if you follow our carefully designed marketing strategy and transaction process.

I call this a Million Dollar Win-Win Home Saver Strategy.

It starts with effective marketing. Your marketing must emphasize that you're not there to purchase the property, but help them resolve their problems.

In simple terms, you will be establishing a new second or first mortgage against the property using privately created funds. Our advanced training can also show you where to get all the money you can use to do these with.

You will use these private funds to pay off any back payments, wipe out any existing liens against the property, such as a second mortgage, taxes due, etc. You can also pay off any other expenses that could impact the property such as insurance, minor repairs or other small judgments. Your goal is to eventually clean up the situation just enough, so that these clients can then qualify for a new first mortgage, to refinance the old first mortgage and this new temporary 2nd mortgage.

The private loan will pay off everything, but may not pay off the first mortgage in many instances. The key is to be certain that, after this new mortgage is in place, there is still at least 30% net equity remaining in the property.

Here is the best part...the part where you make money!

Included in this new mortgage that you're going to create, you'll reserve a "guarantee fee," where you will earn from $7000 to $15,000 each. This is real cash that goes directly into your pocket as a fee for guaranteeing this loan. You will actually be guaranteeing this loan to the private lender. For this guarantee, the lender gets a greater reason to make the loan, and you set up a situation where you are very secure and get paid well for it.

Yes, you are going to guarantee this loan to the private lender...and get paid well for it. Plus, you have a chance to end up owning the property in some cases, with substantial equity, if the owner does not perform as agreed.

The private lender is not likely to make the loan to this home seller without it. But let me show you how there is very little risk to you in doing so.

I will show you, later in this material, a strategy where you can be the guarantor of this loan, and be in an excellent position to actually own the property, if the occupant fails to pay. Therefore, you will have earned your fee, plus you'll receive the equity in the property, if they do not pay as agreed.

If you could earn a $15,000 fee now, plus have the opportunity to later pick up $40,000 to $60,000 in equity (should the occupant not pay as agreed), would you be willing to guarantee that loan?

Give me this deal all day long. I am the lowest risk investor you'll ever find. I understand how to set this transaction up in such a way that I am an absolute minimal risk. My intention is never to take the home if I can avoid it. I want these people to succeed. But if they fail to perform as agreed, the property becomes mine in exchange for the fee and risk assumed for them.

This strategy assumes certain conditions exist:

1. The homeowner has a very low loan to value (LTV) situation. These are the homeowners who don't want to sell to investors anyway, yet may not be able to get a refinance loan to fix their problems.

2. The homeowner has corrected the problem that started the problem. If they lost a job several months ago and got behind, and have since re-established employment satisfactory to make payments, we love that situation. If they have a long history of not making their payments, or criminal background, you may want to stay away from that one.

3. The homeowner cannot qualify for financing due to being currently delinquent on their mortgage. If someone is currently behind on the loan, that is nearly the kiss of death for most institutional lenders. They may offer the world in terms of "easy financing', but come down to it, if you are currently late and everything else is not perfect, "you ain't gettin' the loan."

This entire strategy fulfills a niche for those who need a temporary fix. Further, once their finances are better caught up and credit improved, it will be much easier for the homeowner to go and get a new refinance loan, which will wrap up everything. You will then be paying off the old first mortgage and the new private second mortgage.

At this point, your private investor has their money back safely, PLUS interest, with interest paid at somewhere around 12 to 18 percent return. Best of all, you have been paid your fees up front. Maybe the most rewarding event of all, the homeowners kept their house and re-established their credit.

By the way, if you think the homeowner may object to the original fee charge, think again. What are their other options? Sell and lose their equity, sell or lease back and lose half their equity, or go through this process and give up fewer dollars in fees to keep their equity and improve their credit. If you were faced with these three options, what would you do?

As a "full spectrum" creative investor, you can deal with all three foreclosure circumstances, and everybody wins. But if your approach is strictly from the aspect of getting the property and all the equity, you're going to face a great deal of rejection. So why not approach the business in the reverse direction, to beat the competition?

The Marketing Strategy:

1. Establish some letters and postcards that you will mail to homeowners.

2. Establish a service to get access to properties in pre-foreclosure or potential tax sale foreclosure. I highly recommend the services as we offer through our web site: www.tjmarrs.com .

   Under the Tools link, you'll see a link to get Pre-Foreclosure leads.

3. Download the leads to your computer in a spreadsheet format.

4. Go through the leads and look up Comparable Sales Values for each property, to determine rough equity estimates. You might even establish a column on your spreadsheet to estimate the percent of equity remaining, as compared to the value of the property. Focus your attention on the properties with 35 percent or more equity in them.

5. Direct mail to those properties that appear to have substantial equity. Hit each lead several times. We also suggest that you go out and knock on the doors of these properties to get the best results and to stand out from the crowd. If knocking on doors makes you nervous, just give it a try. It works. Don't be surprised that some people aren't happy to see you, but if you can get your message through to them in a caring and empathetic way, they will thank you. Keep your mission and message in mind. There won't be a huge number of these larger equity situations to deal with on a weekly basis, compared to the whole list. So you'll find that driving by several of them won't take a large amount of time, but it will be very financially rewarding to make this extra effort.

6. While you are out there, carry some flyers to describe how your services different from the rest and include a business card. Post these on the door of any house which is vacant or where no one is home.

Other marketing strategies that have proven to work in this situation:

Loan broker and realtor referrals:

Make a habit of visiting with different mortgage brokers and realtors every week. They work with people in these situations on a constant basis. The very first referral I ever got with this strategy came from a Realtor who just wants to help someone out.

Mortgage brokers turn people down in these situations every day, and they are among the first people who will know people who could really use our plan. Carefully explain to them what you offer and explain what your criteria are. They will send excellent leads. My best students get most other businesses from these referrals, in addition to the leads obtained by a highly targeted direct mail campaign.

There are literally about 35 different ways to locate motivated and distressed homeowners, but this third strategy (providing private financing) works best with these two Reverse Foreclosure strategies that we have shared with you. You should become familiar with those 35 different strategies, because there are many more ways to make money in real estate, if you understand them. There are great deals all over out there, and you need to become a transaction engineer in order to profit from them.

So How Do You Make REAL Money at This?

Once you have a homeowner who has accepted your offer to create a private loan to wrap up all of their bad debt problems, you need a closing strategy where you'll get paid.

How do you think you'll feel while earning a quick **$10,000 to $15,000** to **2-3 times a month**? Not a bad income! "Ya gotta make a livin."

The primary instrument you'll use to get paid and to create a private loan is a promissory note, combined with a trust deed (or a mortgage, in states which choose mortgages vs. trust deeds). Consult with a local attorney in setting this portion up.

I strongly advise that you close these transactions with the assistance of an attorney, and charge the fees out of the loan proceeds (not out of your pocket). In other words, this money does not come out of your pocket: it comes out of the homeowner's pocket. It is best to be sure everyone is protected and that you're carefully following local laws in conducting this program.

In many states, if you're construed as offering loans, you may have certain licensing requirements you need to follow, unless you have an effective strategy to avoid it. So what do you call this fee that you will earn? If you do not want to go through a mortgage licensing process, how do you get paid?

Again, I suggest you consult with an attorney in your states with some of the ideas that I will propose.

Avoid being labeled a "lender" if you can.

Here are some ways you might structure your business to avoid being labeled as a lender.

1. Make no mention of a loan or financing in any of your marketing material. You might refer to "get the money you need." But nothing more, until you are sitting one on one with the homeowner.

2. Classify your fee as a "guarantee fee." After all, you are assuming the risk for this homeowner. You should get paid for it. You are not getting paid for a loan fee. You would then simply submit a letter into the escrow when the transaction closes, for your guarantee fee. Be sure to have the home seller sign it. If you cannot come up with something, have your attorney design a letter for the homeowner to sign. It might also be a good idea to include some disclaimers and disclosures, as directed by your attorney.

3. You can also classify your fee as payment for a **Purchase Option Cancellation fee.** When you establish your relationship with this homeowner, establish a purchase option agreement, and record a "memorandum of agreement" in the county records. This memorandum will have to be removed prior to any creation of a new loan against the property. You are simply being paid for your option cancellation. The stated purchase price in the option agreement would equal the balances due on their existing loans. Your agreement would also contain a cancellation fee clause, in exchange for removing the cloud on the title. You then get paid at closing for the new private mortgage. This cancellation fee could be from $7,000 to $15,000!

   With this strategy, you are simply an investor who is being paid the cancellation fee. I use a cancellation fee as a standard paragraph in all of my option agreements, whether it is in one of these private loan scenarios or not.

NOTE: A standard set of forms, complete with the promissory note language, and the option agreement example, are part of our full course packages. Use of these pre-established forms could dramatically reduce your legal costs and time in getting started.

FREE REPORT:
**Where to get more money that you can handle
to fund your deals**

At this point you might be thinking...So, I just have to find people in foreclosure who will sell to me using these creative approaches. But where will I find someone who would make such quick loans to buy them with?

My answerer is: Don't trip over all the cash available, while pacing around your neighborhood, thinking about it.

I can hear the "doubters" out there already. Let me assure you; there are many people in this world who would love to earn a higher return on their money than 3%-5% currently offered by banks and money market funds.

It is estimated that there is $4.7 trillion sitting in IRAs and CDs earning less than 4-5% interest in this country. Many of these folks NEED to earn a greater return in order to just survive today. Of course, they don't want to take unnecessary risks. So they can follow our special plan.

A recent study in *Business Week* magazine notes that there is a glut of cash in the world looking for a home, and cash LOVES real estate!

With the right approach and plan, you'll be amazed how many people would step up with money when you need it, more than you can handle – once they understand that you structure a deal in such a way that they can double their returns, all while protected by solid equity PLUS your personal guarantee.

The first key is, have a personalized and professional approach. In many states, you cannot simply advertise that you are seeking money to invest with, without stepping into a hornet's nest regarding securities solicitation. Again, ask your local attorney about rules you should consider.

Start by asking around. Get referrals. Networking is the best solution for finding money. Use these words a lot "who do you know..."

For example:

"Who do you know who might have some cash sitting around earning less than 4% to 5% per year? We are developing some safe real estate investment strategies, where we will pay 12% to 18% for the use of that money. We're secured by plenty of equity."

Ask your friends, relatives, accountant, attorney, mortgage broker, Realtor, etc. Remember do ask them "who they know." Never ask, "Do you know?" You'll be amazed that what a systematic effort can attain.

You could also hold a luncheon, if you know some investment advisers who might want to work with you. Explain to these investment advisers what you do, and ask if they would be interested in assisting you in offering a luncheon. At this luncheon, you might prepare a small presentation with some handouts and an application form. You simply explain how safe equity is and how you personally guarantee the loan, even if it is really not needed. Close the deal by asking if they would rather keep earning 3% to 4%, or 12% to 18% secured with equity? Always remind people that all that you are asking them to do is submit their name to be contacted, if and when opportunities arise.

Be sure to remind these people that they can also use their IRA funds, or 401(k) funds for these deals. They may need to first place their funds with a custodian who does not mind allowing them to place funds in real estate deals. Many traditional IRA custodians will limit their clients to stocks and bonds they offer. Remember, it is your money, and it is legal to place your IRA funds into real estate or private loans, if you follow IRS regulations. A custodian who specializes in real estate will not argue with you about it. They would help you comply with your own wishes.

A custodian I really like working with is called Entrust. They have offices in multiple states. There is likely an office near you. Go to www.iraplus.com to research them. They can help you get funds placed into self-directed account easily.

On average, a luncheon with 10 or more participants can produce over $1 million in available funds for your own little private bank to use. There is plenty of cash out there if you make the effort.

Be sure to get enrolled in our newsletter at: www.tjmarrs.com
to find out how to get more free and advanced training on this soon.

Resource Directory
Advanced Tools of the Trade to Save You Both Time and Money

Pay your mortgage debt off in 7 - 8 years vs. 30, without significantly changing your budget. Yes, really!

Get details at: www.livefreeandclear.com
Get out of debt and into wealth much faster with this system.

Get Legal Services You'll Need FAST, and Save Money at the Same Time: Do you think you'll ever want to hire an attorney, but don't want the costs? With Prepaid legal, you'll always be working with top-rated attorneys, at a fraction of the cost of regular attorneys services. I pay upwards of about $26-$69 a month for most of my legal service needs. Most of you pay over $200 an hour for the same services. Do what I do.

Please join me via my prepaid legal web site link to sign up at:
http://www.prepaidlegal.com/hub/assets
You'll also find many of the people you want to help need legal services themselves and could save substantially by being a member of prepaid legal. Why am I telling you this? You can also sign up as an associate and earn a substantial income every time someone signs up.
Get details on joining my team at:
http://www.prepaidlegal.com/hub/assets

Self-Directed IRAs:

You'll need a custodian who is friendly about allowing you, as a real estate investor, to invest in real estate. Visit www.tjmarrs.com for special links and tools.

Support your investing income by doing some mortgages, as a part or full time loan officer. Top earners earn $50,000- $250,000 PER MONTH (yes, really) with our unique compensation plan. Go to: www.mynlc.com Use referral code: **A33490**

Pre Foreclosure Leads and Property Research Tools:

Go to www.tjmarrs.com, go to the "Tools link," and pull down the pre-foreclosures leads link for a free trial. After that, you only invest about $20-$30 a month to continue to receive all the leads you can handle.

More training and education:

Visit www.tjmarrs.com for details on workshops, seminars, and coaching, so you can get to the serious level of investing much faster.

Coaching Questionnaire from T.J. Marrs

Could you qualify to get a personal coach to help you get to the next level?

1) How many deals do you <u>want</u> to do this year?

2) Will having a coach <u>increase</u> your success on doing these deals?

3) Do you have the <u>skills and resources</u> at this moment to do the number of deals in question 2?

4) Do you have the <u>confidence</u> to do the number of deals in question one without help?

5) If I were your coach, <u>what could I do to</u> help you do the number of deals in question one?

6) How much money would you like to <u>earn</u> from each deal?

7) Do you believe that having an experienced coach can help you <u>achieve your financial goal faster</u>?

8) Do you know of <u>other situations</u> in life where a coach has helped keep someone of high achievement reach their goals?

9) What is the <u>potential cost of making a mistake</u> in real estate investing?

10) When is the best time to <u>take action</u> to change your future now or later?

11) If price were not a factor, what would stop you from <u>starting now</u>?

12) If we could make the payment plan <u>comfortable</u>, are you willing to commit to yourself to start now?

Name _____ Email_____ Phone# _____

Fax to 360-397-0159 or email your responses to:
questionsfortj@creclub.com
Ph 360-883-2296 www.creclub.com   www.livingfreeandclear.com

Glossary of Terms

27-Year Depreciation – An accounting deduction that allows a property owner to deduct certain expenses involved with the normal wear and tear of a non-owner occupied property. Typically, the building itself and some fixtures may be "depreciated."

Assumable Loans – A mortgage that may be transferred to another party upon bank approval of the other party. These are rare today.

Bank Qualified – The process of getting formal "bank" approval or pre-approval from a lending institution, to purchase a home.

Bank-Owned Properties – A post foreclosure auction property. These are properties that have already been foreclosed upon by a mortgagor and have returned to the mortgagor's possession and control. These mortgagors typically do not want to own these homes.

Binder Payment – A non-refundable payment in exchange for the right to purchase real estate. This usually comes from a tenant/buyer, typically in consideration for the option to purchase a property.

Cash Flow – Monthly net income on an investment property after expenses.

Deed – The document that represents the transfer of legal title to a property.

Deeply Discounted – For a variety of reasons, a property or a note that can be bought at a price significantly below real market value or face value.

Double Close – An escrow transaction where 2 transactions happen almost simultaneously. In this situation, Party "A" sells a property to Party

"B." Party "B" then finds Party "C" to purchase the same property at a higher value. At closing, "C" brings money, some of which will go to "A" as "A" relinquishes title to the property. "B" then collects the monetary difference in sale prices. "B" technically owns the property for a very short period of time (on paper) before turning around and selling to "C." **Equity** – The "net" dollars remaining after a seller sells a property. It is also represented as the difference between the real market value of a property and the balance of the debt owed against the property.

Exchanges – A transaction which allows the seller to defer taxes due, in effect, because their intent is to ultimately exchange their equity into another property by a specified time. Formally called a [Internal Revenue Code] Section 1031 tax exchange. The proceeds from the original property may be used in their entirety to purchase the new property(ies) without immediate tax penalty.

Exercise an Option – The final decision to exercise a right to by property, as contractually agreed to in an option agreement.

Fixer Upper Property – Sometimes just called a "fixer," this is a property that requires a significant amount of repair, before it can be sold at a full market retail value.

Foreclosure – The final process of a mortgage holder taking back a property, when the mortgage has not been paid as agreed. The lender reclaims possession of a property upon which they lent money. This typically happens during a public auction proceeding.

Friendly Corporation – A corporation that does business with you or your local in-state corporation. You are in total control of this corporation privately. This may give you an advantage of creating protective liens against your own properties for asset protection purposes.

IRA/Individual Retirement Account – A tax-deferred way to save money for retirement. In a ROTH IRA account, taxes are paid upon deposit into the account, so that no taxes are due upon retirement. Most other IRAs are tax deferred until retirement.

Lease Option – A lease agreement with an option to buy the same property. Typically, a buyer will sign an agreement to lease a given property with the intention to purchase that property. An option is a unilateral agreement stating that the buyer may buy the property if they choose, and the seller must sell the property, if the buyer makes the choice to buy.

Pre-Foreclosure – A property headed toward foreclosure soon. It begins with the period of time between when a mortgage holder gives notice (usually called a "Notice of Default") and completes the foreclosure process, usually through a public auction. The mortgagee (property owner on title) retains the right to sell the property and pay off the mortgage holder during this time.

Probate – In most cases, this happens after one is deceased, as the process to ensure all creditors are given an opportunity to make claims against an estate.

Real Estate Trust / Land Trust – A special property-only trust. Considered a protective entity, it is used to hold title to property and create a situation in which benefits of ownership may be easily transferred more privately.

Residual Income – Income earned from investments or other sources which pay ongoing income after established. This is as opposed to wages earned through paid or self-employment.

Retailing – The process of buying property below market value and selling at full retail market value.

Sandwich Lease Option – The position being between two lease option transactions. One first purchases a property on a lease with the option to buy, then turns around and sub-leases the property to another party, at a higher payment and terms, hopefully. The final buyer also has an option to buy (typically at a higher cost than paid to the original seller).

Straight Option – The right to buy, but not the obligation to do so, as in a purchase agreement. It is a unilateral agreement stating that the buyer may buy the property if they choose and the seller must sell the property if the buyer makes the choice to buy.

Subject to – An alternative to "assuming" a loan. One is simply taking over a seller's mortgage "payments," leaving the existing financing in place (and in the seller's name).

Tax deferral – Any transaction that allows for a deferral of what would normally be immediate taxes. When a tax debt is owed, it is a legal way to put that debt on hold, sometimes indefinitely. Most typically utilized through IRA accounts and exchanges.

Tenant/Buyer – An individual leasing a property with the intention (and option) to purchase the property sometime in the future.

Unilateral – A contract agreement where only one party is obligated to complete some action.
Wholesaling – The process of acquiring property below market value, then selling at a higher value, yet still below full retail market value.

Wrap around – Any transaction whereby an underlying loan is being paid by a new "wrap around" larger note. This is the process of using underlying financing to extend financing to a potential buyer.

Zero down – Any process where one purchases property with no cash down or using other people's money as a down payment.

EXAMPLE PURCHASE FORMS

ADDITIONAL FORMS CAN BE FOUND IN OUR ADVANCED COURSES.

General Checklist For Buying Houses

Property I.D.: _____

___ Phone worksheet summary - completed with seller's help
___ Complete Deal Analysis/Submission Spreadsheet
___ Signed contract; purchase agreement, option, or lease option agreement, and addendums
___ Comparables (comps) sold within the last 6 months, within .25 miles preferred.
___ Seller disclosure/disclaimer/addendum (i.e.: long, short, lease opt, etc)
___ Lead Paint disclosure
___ Smoke alarm disclosure
___ Closing documents
___ Current 1st trust deed and note   ___2nd ___3rd
___ Last 2 months mortgage statements   ___1st ___ 2nd ___3rd
___ Authorization to Release Loan Information Form
___ Last month Gas Bill   ___ Last month Water/sewer bill   ___Last month electric bill
___ Last HOA statement (Home Owners Association, if any)
___ Last home owners insurance statement
___ 3 Estimates of repairs from licensed contractors (if a fixer)
___ Most recent property tax statements
___ Title Report. You may start with a "lien and encumbrance" report to save money until transaction gets more serious.
___ Signed Excise tax affidavit form (if in excise tax states)
___ IRS lien check on seller - get seller credit authorization to do so
___ City lien check for sewer and water issues or other issues (title report may help)
___ Judgment check on seller (title report may help)
___ Seller's name, DOB, SSN and signed authorization to verify information
___ Property condition checklist / disclosure signed by seller
___ Any special checklists we included in our specialty courses

If Buying "Subject To"

____ Check on any local issues relating to using a trust, ie: your state or title company may require a filing of a business trust or similar filing, and the possible required use of escrow for the transaction to ensure you don't cloud title for re-sale later. If you prefer , you can simply deed the property directly to your company or to yourself, especially if you may be refinancing soon.

    ____ If using a Land trust prepare and sign: ____ Trust agreement

    ____ Warrantee Deed ____Assignment.

____ OPTIONAL WITH TRUSTS: Bill of Sale for Beneficial interest, an a trust disclosure addendum

Otherwise, in all cases:

____ Warrantee Deed: Unto the trustee or to you or your company as applicable.

____ Due on Sale Disclosure outlining there is an underlying loan and what happens if called.

____ Special Power of Attorney signed by seller, for all business relating to the property, mortgage, or insurance.

____ Letter to banks signed by seller regarding power of attorney to managing the property and loan.

____ Letter to insurance company regarding adding you or your trustee as loss payee.

If not using a trust, it should list your company or personal name.

If Buying using Single Escrow Flip or Holding in escrow for a lease option or contract:

____ **Warrantee Deed:** Leave buyer name blank for now until YOUR buyer closes, if holding transaction in escrow – See single escrow flip section.

____ **Promissory Note & Deed of Trust** to secure the equity and performance by the seller (usually used for Land contract or lease option purchases).

____ If a Deed of Trust from the seller is not possible, us a **Memorandum or Affidavit of Agreement** to cloud title in your favor.

____ **Special Power of Attorney** signed by seller - for all business relating to the property.

For Buying on a Lease Option (in addition to above):

____ **Lease-Option Agreement:** Single contract format when buying, in addition to a Purchase agreement.

____ **Authorization to Release Information:** To verify loan balances by phone or fax

____ **Memorandum or Affidavit of Option:** To record your option and protect your interest.

____ **Lead Hazard Disclosure from Seller to You** ___ Plus receive a booklet/flyer on lead hazard.

____ **Preliminary Title Report** or Lien and Encumbrance report

____ **Performance Promissory Note & Deed of Trust** (or mortgage-in mortgage states), to guarantee and protect sellers title and performance to you.

For Buying on Option:

____ **Option Agreement** (buying version) or a modified Standard Purchase Agreement.

____ May use a **modified purchase agreement** "subject to buyer (you the investor) securing their buyer"

____ **Memorandum or Affidavit of Option**, to protect your interest with a recorded document, by clouding title.

____ Pay smallest amount of **option money** as possible (i.e.: $10-$100)

____ OPTIONAL: Get a **performance promissory note & Deed of Trust** from seller to you; for protection of your interest and payment later when you re-sell. See Single Escrow Flip section.

For Purchase or Selling on Installment Land Contract,
see that special course checklist or seek legal counsel in your area.
Post Purchase Checklist - Property Preparation
Start this the moment you get a property under contract

Property I.D.:

_____ Install your "For Sale" sign post with a flyer box.

_____ Install "For sale" sign in front of property, with FLYERS which also reference your other properties, and web site.

_____ Install several "directional arrow signs" in the area, to lead buyers in.

_____ Put up your separate "I buy homes" sign in the yard.

_____ Transfer and set up utilities: water, electricity, gas, etc
_____ Record new messages on you selling voice mail system to screen calls, then give your direct number to call there.

_____ On your web site: Post pictures and flyer, with a downloadable flyers they can print along with a map.

_____ Add the house and "numbers" information to your master sales list, for easy reference.

_____ Cut grass and landscape first, street appeal is the first thing to address.

_____ Complete schedule of repairs and clean and stage worksheet. Do this ASAP. Time IS money here.

_____ Get the proper ad running to advertise the property, and keep it running.

_____ Run direct mail campaign to same zip code or get a kid to pass out flyers to neighborhood

____ Confirm 1st mailing _____number mailed 2nd mailing date on
_____.

Target renters who match your houses for sale. Hopefully you started a buyer list earlier as well.

____ Compile a Voice Mail Lead Tracking Evaluation Sheet for Weekly review.

____ Prepare: spreadsheet "short cut showing buying options", plus have underlying loan information on it, for easy reference. Keep a copy with you, your assistant, and at the property.

____ Possibly list in MLS with discount listing services, if you intend on selling faster.

____ Have all of your selling forms applicable on site as well as on your person.

____ Start a Closing Folder for the applicant, once application receipt is taken.

____ Get a second applicant lined up with a deposit, as a backup.

Standard Purchase and Purchase Option Forms
Used for buying most properties, creating options, and assigning them.

Index

- AGREEMENT FOR PURCHASE & SALE OF REAL ESTATE (PURCHASE AGREEMENT)
- **AUTHORIZATION TO RELEASE INFORMATION (TO GET TITLE AND LENDER INFO)**
- PURCHASE AGREEMENT ADDENDUM AND UNDERSTANDING (DISCLOSURE)
- AFFIDAVIT AND MEMORANDUM OF AGREEMENT CONCERNING REAL ESTATE (TO SECURE YOUR POSITION AND CLOUD TITLE IN YOUR FAVOR - RECORD THIS)
- OPTION TO PURCHASE REAL ESTATE AGREEMENT (OPTION TO SECURING YOUR POSITION IF PURCHASE AGREEMENT DOES NOT WORK)
- ASSIGNMENT OF CONTRACT (TO ASSIGN YOUR POSITION FOR A FEE)
- DEFINITION OF "EQUITY" AND YOUR SELLING OPTIONS (TO CLOSE SELLERS ON YOUR "SUBJECT TO" OR OTHER OFFER REDUCED PRICE)
- WARRANTY DEED (TRANSFERS TITLE QUICKLY – RECORD THIS)
- NOTICE TO THE BUYER

3. PURCHASE AGREEMENTS FOLLOW - STANDARD FORMAT, SUBJECT TO, AND OWNER FINANCING. FOR LEASE OPTION PURCHASES, USE THE LEASE OPTION FORMS AS A PURCHASE AGREEMENT. OR SIMPLY USE THIS FORM INITIALLY SPELLING OUT THE TERMS OF THE LEASE OPTION.

These are common documents used, and may not necessarily represent every document for every transaction. Consult professional legal counsel for review of these documents or any documents you may use to real estate transactions. These are not necessarily approved for legal use. Other possible documents may be found in our general documents folder.

AGREEMENT FOR PURCHASE & SALE OF REAL ESTATE
(PB rev. 01172004)

AGREEMENT dated this ___ day of _____,_200__ by and between **Joe Seller AND Jane Seller**_hereinafter "Seller" whose address is **123 Anywhere street, Omaha, NB 99889** and **Joe Investor** hereinafter "Buyer" whose address : **233 Smith street, Vancouver, WA 99008** .

1. THE PROPERTY. The parties hereby agree that Seller will sell and Buyer will buy the following property, located in and situate in the County of **Multnomah**, State of **Oregon** , known by street and address as **555 Forest street, Portland, OR 99889** more particularly described as follows (enter legal description below):

5th Block of the last piece of dirt in Portland

The sale shall also include all personal property and fixtures, ___except _x__ including: refrigerator & stove

_____

_____.

Unless specifically excluded, all other items will be included, whether or not affixed to the property or structures. Seller expressly warrants that property, improvements, building or structures, the appliances, roof, plumbing, heating and/or ventilation systems are in good and working order. This clause shall survive closing of title.

2 PURCHASE PRICE. The total purchase price to be paid by Buyer will be payable as follows:

Earnest money deposit or note (see below)	$100
Owner financing from seller (see below) _____	$0
New loan (see below)	$150,000
'Subject to' existing loan(s) with _____	of approx.
	$_____
Cash balance due at closing	$_____
Total Purchase Price and/or Consideration	$150,100

____ Sale price not to exceed acceptable existing lender payoffs, as determined by buyer.

_X_ Said price is subject to appraisal by buyer and/or agent of buyer's choice.

___ The agreement only gives the buyer a ____ day ____exclusive / ___ non exclusive right to purchase.

3. EARNEST MONEY. The buyer's earnest money shall be held in escrow by agent of buyer's choice. Upon default of this agreement, seller shall retain earnest money as his sole remedy without further recourse between the parties.

4. NEW LOAN. This agreement is contingent upon buyer's ability to obtain a new loan in the amount of $150,000. Buyer is not required to accept any loan with interest rate exceeding 8% amortized over 30 years or pay any closing costs or points exceeding $3,000. Buyer shall provide seller with written proof of a loan commitment on or before_____, 200__.

5. SELLER FINANCING. Buyer shall execute a promissory note in the amount of $_____. In case of default, recourse shall be against the property an there shall be no personal recourse against the borrower. As security for performance of the promissory note, buyer shall provide the seller a mortgage, deed of trust or other customary security agreement which shall be subordinate to a new or current first mortgage not to exceed $_____.

6. EXISTING LOAN. In the event part of the purchase price is to be satisfied by buyer taking subject to existing financing, buyer shall not be required to pay fees exceeding $_____ nor be required to show income or creditworthiness to the holder of said mortgage or deed of trust. Seller expressly agrees and understands that buyer is taking the property "subject to" such mortgages or deeds of trust, and is not expressly assuming responsibility for the underlying loans. If the actual loan balance of said loan is less than as stated herein, the purchase price shall be reduced to reflect the difference; if the actual loan balance is more than as stated herein, then buyer's required cash payment shall be reduced accordingly. Seller agrees to waive tax and insurance escrows held by said lender or its/assigns.
Payments to begin _____, 200__ the month end payment for _____, 200__

7. CLOSING. Closing will held be on or about _____200__, at a time and place designated by buyer. Buyer shall choose the escrow, title and/or closing agent. Buyer may assign or substitute this agreement at closing for valuable consideration, seller may then close with the new buyer, with same proceeds originally agreed to going to seller.

Seller agrees to convey title by a general warranty deed. Buyer shall pay the following costs in transferring title:

[X] title insurance policy [ ] loan assumption [X] transfer fee [X] transfer taxes [X] recording fees [X] title company closing, escrow and delivery charges [X] hazard insurance premium [ ] mortgage insurance premium [ ] survey [ ] credit application.

The following Items _x__ will / ___will not be prorated at closing: [X] Mortgage insurance   [X] Property taxes   [ ] PMI Insurance   [ ] Hazard insurance   [ ] Homeowner's association dues   [ ] Rents   [ ] Other _____ **(THIS DEPENDS ON IF YOU CAN GAIN SOMETHING)**

The buyer may extend the closing date an additional __30___ days by paying the seller **$1,000** in cash.
Buyer reserves the right to do a final "walk through" the day of closing.

8.   POSSESSION. Seller shall surrender possession to the property in broom clean condition, and free of all personal items and debris on or before _____200__ ("possession date", In the event possession is not delivered at closing, buyer shall withhold proceeds from the sale in the amount of **$5,000** as security. Seller shall be liable for damages in the amount of $_____ per day for each day the property is occupied beyond the possession date.
This paragraph shall survive the closing of title.

9.   INSPECTION. This agreement is subject to the final inspection and approval of the property by the buyer in writing on or before _____, 200__.

10. ACCESS. Buyer shall be entitled a key and be entitled to access to show partners, lenders, inspectors and/or contractors prior to closing.   Buyer may place an appropriate sign on the property prior to closing for prospective tenants, contractors and/or assigns.

11. SECURING THIS AGREEMENT. Buyer _X_may __ may not record additional instruments necessary to secure sellers performance, protect the title, ensure and delivery of title and closing as necessary. Seller agrees to sign such documents as necessary to meet buyer's purchasing requirements and to close more efficiently. These documents may include:
__ Deed of Trust   __ Promissory note   __ Other lien instruments   _X__Sellers executed deed held in escrow
Other _____

OTHER PROVISIONS AND CONDITIONS: See addendum or exhibit ___

_____
_____

_____
_____

X_____   _____200_
Seller: Joe Seller

X_____   _____200_
Seller: Jane Seller

X_____   _____200_
Buyer: Joe Investor

AGREEMENT FOR PURCHASE & SALE OF REAL ESTATE
SUBJECT TO EXAMPLE

AGREEMENT dated this ___ day of _____,_200__ by and between **Joe Seller AND Jane Seller** hereinafter "Seller" whose address is **123 Anywhere street, Omaha, NB 99889** and **Joe Investor** hereinafter "Buyer" whose address : **233 Smith street, Vancouver, WA 99008** .

      1. THE PROPERTY. The parties hereby agree that Seller will sell and Buyer will buy the following property, located in and situate in the County of **Multnomah**, State of **Oregon** , known by street and address as **555 Forest street, Portland, OR 99889**
      more particularly described as follows (enter legal description below):
5th Block of the last piece of dirt in Portland

The sale shall also include all personal property and fixtures, ___except

_x__ including: **refrigerator & stove**

_____

_____.

Unless specifically excluded, all other items will be included, whether or not affixed to the property or structures. Seller expressly warrants that property, improvements, building or structures, the appliances, roof, plumbing, heating and/or ventilation systems are in good and working order. This clause shall survive closing of title.

      2. PURCHASE PRICE. The total purchase price to be paid by Buyer will be payable as follows:

Earnest money deposit or note (see below)	$100
Owner financing from seller (see below) _____	$0
New loan (see below)	$_____
'Subject to' existing loan(s) with FIRST AM MORTGAGE of approx.	$160,000
Cash balance due at closing	$10,000
Total Purchase Price and/or Consideration	$170,100

_X_   Sale price not to exceed acceptable existing lender payoffs, as determined by buyer.
_X_   Said price is subject to appraisal by buyer and/or agent of buyer's choice.

___ The agreement only gives the buyer a ____ day ____exclusive / ___ non exclusive right to purchase.

3. EARNEST MONEY. The buyer's earnest money shall be held in escrow by agent of buyer's choice. Upon default of this agreement, seller shall retain earnest money as his sole remedy without further recourse between the parties.

4. NEW LOAN. This agreement is contingent upon buyer's ability to obtain a new loan in the amount of $_____. Buyer is not required to accept any loan with interest rate exceeding _____% amortized over _____ years or pay any closing costs or points exceeding $3,000. Buyer shall provide seller with written proof of a loan commitment on or before_____, 200__.

5. SELLER FINANCING. Buyer shall execute a promissory note in the amount of $_____. In case of default, recourse shall be against the property an there shall be no personal recourse against the borrower. As security for performance of the promissory note, buyer shall provide the seller a mortgage, deed of trust or other customary security agreement which shall be subordinate to a new or current first mortgage not to exceed $_____.

6. EXISTING LOAN. In the event part of the purchase price is to be satisfied by buyer taking subject to existing financing, buyer shall not be required to pay fees exceeding $0 nor be required to show income or creditworthiness to the holder of said mortgage or deed of trust. Seller expressly agrees and understands that buyer is taking the property "subject to" such mortgages or deeds of trust, and is not expressly assuming responsibility for the underlying loans. If the actual loan balance of said loan is less than as stated herein, the purchase price shall be reduced to reflect the difference; if the actual loan balance is more than as stated herein, then buyer's required cash payment shall be reduced accordingly. Seller agrees to waive tax and insurance escrows held by said lender or its/assigns.

Payments to begin ____YOU DECIDE_____, 200__ the month end payment for _____, 200__

7. CLOSING. Closing will held be on or about _____200__, at a time and place designated by buyer. Buyer shall choose the escrow, title and/or closing agent. Buyer may assign or substitute this agreement at closing for valuable consideration, seller may then close with the new buyer, with same proceeds originally agreed to going to seller.

Seller agrees to convey title by a general warranty deed. Buyer shall pay the following costs in transferring title:

[X] title insurance policy   [ ] loan assumption   [X] transfer fee   [X] transfer taxes [X] recording fees   [X] title company closing, escrow and delivery charges [X] hazard insurance premium   [ ] mortgage insurance premium [ ] survey [ ] credit application.

The following Items ___ will / _**X**__will not be prorated at closing: [X] Mortgage insurance   [X] Property taxes   [ ] PMI Insurance   [ ] Hazard insurance   [ ] Homeowner's association dues   [ ] Rents   [ ] Other _____ (**THIS DEPENDS ON IF YOU CAN GAIN SOMETHING**)

The buyer may extend the closing date an additional __**30**___ days by paying the seller **$1,000** in cash.
Buyer reserves the right to do a final "walk through" the day of closing.
      8.   POSSESSION.   Seller shall surrender possession to the property in broom clean condition, and free of all personal items and debris on or before _____200__ ("possession date", In the event possession is not delivered at closing, buyer shall withhold proceeds from the sale in the amount of $5,000 as security. Seller shall be liable for damages in the amount of $_____ per day for each day the property is occupied beyond the possession date.
      This paragraph shall survive the closing of title.

      9.   INSPECTION.   This agreement is subject to the final inspection and approval of the property by the buyer in writing on or before _____, 200__ .

      10.   ACCESS. Buyer shall be entitled a key and be entitled to access to show partners, lenders, inspectors and/or contractors prior to closing.   Buyer may place an appropriate sign on the property prior to closing for prospective tenants, contractors and/or assigns.

      11.   SECURING THIS AGREEMENT.   Buyer _X_may __ may not record additional instruments necessary to secure sellers performance, protect the title, ensure and delivery of title and closing as necessary. Seller agrees to sign such documents as necessary to meet buyer's purchasing requirements and to close more efficiently.   These documents may include:
    __ Deed of Trust   __ Promissory note   _X_ Other lien instruments
  _X__Sellers executed deed held in escrow
    Other _____

OTHER PROVISIONS AND CONDITIONS: See addendum or exhibit ___

_____
_____

_____
_____

X_____   _____ 200_
Seller: Joe Seller

X_____   _____ 200_
Seller: Jane Seller

X_____   _____ 200_
Buyer: Joe Investor

AGREEMENT FOR PURCHASE & SALE OF REAL ESTATE
INSTALLMENT CONTRACT EXAMPLE

AGREEMENT dated this ___ day of _____,200__ by and between **Joe Seller AND Jane Seller** hereinafter "Seller" whose address is **123 Anywhere street, Omaha, NB 99889** and **Joe Investor** hereinafter "Buyer" whose address : **233 Smith street, Vancouver, WA 99008** .

      1.   THE PROPERTY. The parties hereby agree that Seller will sell and Buyer will buy the following property, located in and situate in the County of **Multnomah**, State of **Oregon** , known by street and address as **555 Forest street, Portland, OR 99889**
      more particularly described as follows (enter legal description below):
5th Block of the last piece of dirt in Portland

The sale shall also include all personal property and fixtures, ___except

_x__ including: **refrigerator & stove**

_____

_____.

      Unless specifically excluded, all other items will be included, whether or not affixed to the property or structures.   Seller expressly warrants that property, improvements, building or structures, the appliances, roof, plumbing, heating and/or ventilation systems are in good and working order. This clause shall survive closing of title.

      2.   PURCHASE PRICE. The total purchase price to be paid by Buyer will be payable as follows:

Earnest money deposit or note (see below)	$100
Owner financing from seller (see below) _____	$140,000
New loan (see below)	$_____
'Subject to" existing loan(s) with FIRST AM MORTGAGE of approx.	$_____
Cash balance due at closing	$15,000
Total Purchase Price and/or Consideration	$155,100

_X_   Sale price not to exceed acceptable existing lender payoffs, as determined by buyer.
_X_   Said price is subject to appraisal by buyer and/or agent of buyer's choice.

____ The agreement only gives the buyer a _____ day _____exclusive / ____ non exclusive right to purchase.

3. EARNEST MONEY. The buyer's earnest money shall be held in escrow by agent of buyer's choice. Upon default of this agreement, seller shall retain earnest money as his sole remedy without further recourse between the parties.

4. NEW LOAN. This agreement is contingent upon buyer's ability to obtain a new loan in the amount of $_____. Buyer is not required to accept any loan with interest rate exceeding _____% amortized over _____ years or pay any closing costs or points exceeding $_____. Buyer shall provide seller with written proof of a loan commitment on or before_____, 200__.

5. SELLER FINANCING. Buyer shall execute a promissory note in the amount of $140,000. In case of default, recourse shall be against the property an there shall be no personal recourse against the borrower. As security for performance of the promissory note, buyer shall provide the seller a mortgage, deed of trust or other customary security agreement which shall be subordinate to a new or current first mortgage not to exceed $125,000. SEE ADDENDUM FOR ADDITIONAL TERMS OF OWNER FINANCING

6. EXISTING LOAN. In the event part of the purchase price is to be satisfied by buyer taking subject to existing financing, buyer shall not be required to pay fees exceeding $0 nor be required to show income or creditworthiness to the holder of said mortgage or deed of trust. Seller expressly agrees and understands that buyer is taking the property "subject to" such mortgages or deeds of trust, and is not expressly assuming responsibility for the underlying loans. If the actual loan balance of said loan is less than as stated herein, the purchase price shall be reduced to reflect the difference; if the actual loan balance is more than as stated herein, then buyer's required cash payment shall be reduced accordingly. Seller agrees to waive tax and insurance escrows held by said lender or its/assigns.
Payments to begin _____YOU DECIDE_____, 200__ the month end payment for _____, 200__

7. CLOSING. Closing will held be on or about _____200__, at a time and place designated by buyer. Buyer shall choose the escrow, title and/or closing agent. Buyer may assign or substitute this agreement at closing for valuable consideration, seller may then close with the new buyer, with same proceeds originally agreed to going to seller.

Seller agrees to convey title by a general warranty deed. Buyer shall pay the following costs in transferring title:

[X] title insurance policy   [ ] loan assumption   [X] transfer fee   [X] transfer taxes [X] recording fees   [X] title company closing, escrow and delivery charges   [X] hazard insurance premium   [ ] mortgage insurance premium [ ] survey [ ] credit application.

The following Items ___ will / __X__ will not be prorated at closing: [X] Mortgage insurance [X] Property taxes [ ] PMI Insurance [ ] Hazard insurance [ ] Homeowner's association dues [ ] Rents [ ] Other _____ (THIS DEPENDS ON IF YOU CAN GAIN SOMETHING)

The buyer may extend the closing date an additional __30___ days by paying the seller $1,000 in cash.
Buyer reserves the right to do a final "walk through" the day of closing.

8. POSSESSION. Seller shall surrender possession to the property in broom clean condition, and free of all personal items and debris on or before _____200__ ("possession date", In the event possession is not delivered at closing, buyer shall withhold proceeds from the sale in the amount of $5,000 as security. Seller shall be liable for damages in the amount of $_____ per day for each day the property is occupied beyond the possession date.
This paragraph shall survive the closing of title.

9. INSPECTION. This agreement is subject to the final inspection and approval of the property by the buyer in writing on or before _____, 200__.

10. ACCESS. Buyer shall be entitled a key and be entitled to access to show partners, lenders, inspectors and/or contractors prior to closing. Buyer may place an appropriate sign on the property prior to closing for prospective tenants, contractors and/or assigns.

11. SECURING THIS AGREEMENT. Buyer _X_may __ may not record additional instruments necessary to secure sellers performance, protect the title, ensure and delivery of title and closing as necessary. Seller agrees to sign such documents as necessary to meet buyer's purchasing requirements and to close more efficiently. These documents may include:
___ Deed of Trust ___ Promissory note _X_ Other lien instruments _X__Sellers executed deed held in escrow
Other _____

OTHER PROVISIONS AND CONDITIONS: See addendum or exhibit

TERMS OF SELLER FINANCING TO BE A CONTRACT AMOUNT OF $ 140,000 AT 6% ANNUAL RATE, 30 YEAR AMORTIZATION WITH A BALLOON DATE 5 YEARS AFTER CLOSING. PAYMENT NOT TO EXCEED $839.37 P&I PER MONTH.

x_____   _____ 200_
Seller: Joe Seller

x_____   _____ 200_
Seller: Jane Seller

x_____   _____ 200_
Buyer: Joe Investor

Authorization to Release Information

Authorization dated this ____ day of _____, 200__

Borrower(s):   **Joe Seller AND Jane Seller**

Loan No.:   _____

Property: **555 Forest street, Portland, OR 99889**

TO: _____

_____

_____

I/We the undersigned hereby authorize you to release information regarding the above-referenced loan to

Joe Investor   and/or their agents/assigns.

This form may be duplicated in blank and or sent via facsimile transmission. This authorization is a continuation authorization for said persons to receive information about my loan, including duplicates of any notices sent to me regarding my loan.

x_____   DOB:_____
Borrower **Joe Seller**
                                      SSN: _____

x_____   DOB:_____
Borrower **Jane Seller**
                                      SSN: _____

Fax to: 360-397-1100

Purchase Agreement Addendum "_____" and Understanding
REV 0117004 Applicable to Pre-Foreclosure many subject-to offers

As owner of the Real Property known as **555 Forest street, Portland, OR 99889** and, concerning its transfer and conveyance to **Joe Investor** and/or assigns on this date named below, I have been made aware of, understand and agree to the following statements of fact and terms.

    1) **DUE ON SALE CLAUSE OPTION:** That the mortgage on this property contains a "due on sale clause" which means that the lender has the right to call the entire note due and payable upon transfer of title. _____

    2) **MORTGAGE IN NAME OF SELLER:** That the mortgage may stay in owners name until is paid off or assumed by a future known or unknown purchaser. _____

    3) **NOT AN ASSUMPTION:** That the party named above accepting this conveyance has no intentions of assuming said loan and that no promises have been made to owner stating that the loan will be paid off or otherwise assumed or that payments will be made in a timely manner. _____

    4) **PAYMENTS:** That the party accepting this conveyance __has / ___has not agreed to pay any back payments, if any, to remove this property from the perils of foreclosure or default only upon the re-sale of this property. This clause may not apply if certain lender payoff agreements are not acceptably obtained or if certain property conditions prevent funding. No promises have been made to do so prior to that time. _____

    5) **POSSIBILITY OF FORECLOSURE:** That if the party accepting conveyance is unable to sell the property in a timely fashion, owner understands that any other amounts in arrears may not be paid to bring the note current and it may yet go into foreclosure. _____

    6) **HOLD HARMLESS:** That the owner holds the party accepting the conveyance and/or their heirs and assigns or nay future acceptor of this conveyance, harmless and blameless from any debt, action, suit, payment or any liability whatsoever that may be associated in any way with this agreement or of notes, deeds of trust or other liens on this property. _____

    7) **POSSESSION:** Seller shall surrender possession to the property in broom clean condition, and free of all personal items and debris on or before _____, 200__ ("possession date", In the event possession is not delivered at

closing, buyer shall withhold proceeds from the sale in the amount of $_____ as security. Seller shall be liable for damages in the amount of $_____ per day for each day the property is occupied beyond the possession date. This paragraph shall survive closing of title.

8) **INTENT TO PROFIT:** That the seller agrees and understands the buyer intends to profit, amount to be determined, from the purchase and re-sale of subject property. _____

9) **COMMUNICATION:** Seller agrees to stay in communication with buyer and agrees to accept and sign off on any future escrow or other documents as needed to facilitate this transaction, without dispute or delay, when delivered at a future date. Failure to do so is considered a breach of agreement and entitles buyer to exercise their lien position against property through foreclosure procedures, as compensation for damages. _____

10) **FULLY INFORMED AND UNDERSTAND:** I agree that I am fully informed and with sufficient understanding of all terms and conditions contained therein. I am not confused about any aspect of the agreement. _____

11) **SATISFIED WITH THE SALES PRICE:** I understand I may be selling the property for less than market value. I am therefore satisfied with the sales price and terms I have negotiated. _____

12) **LEGAL COUNSEL NOT DENIED:** I acknowledge Buyer has not denied the opportunity to seek independent legal counsel regarding this transaction _____.

13) **FAIRLY NEGOTIATED:** I understand Buyer has negotiated on his own behalf and likewise, I have negotiated on mine. I acknowledge this agreement has been negotiated fairly and Buyer has not taken advantage of me or my current situation, nor is Seller under physical or financial duress, or under the influence of alcohol or other mind influencing drugs at the time of signing. _____

14) **EXECUTION IN COUNTERPARTS:** This agreement may be executed in counterparts and by facsimile signatures. This agreement shall become effective as of the date of the last signature. _____

15) **LEGAL AUTHORITY:** Seller shall provide proof of legal authority to execute this sale. Seller shall also provide evidence property is free of current or future encumbrances or liens from any estate, entities, or persons previously on title to this property, except those disclosed here. _____   **Seller initial**

_____   _____

ADDITIONAL CONDITIONS OF THE OFFER:

Offer is subject to (check which is applicable):

____ This transaction is subject to an inspection by my partner within 3 days of the seller's acceptance of the offer.

____ Subject to purchaser's acceptable negotiation and discount with current lenders who hold liens on subject property.

Other_____

_____

_____

_____

_____

_____

On this ____ day of _____, 20___, we the owners have set our name and seal

X_____   X_____
Seller Signature   Seller Signature
Joe Seller   **Jane Seller**

Affidavit and Memorandum Of
Agreement Concerning Real Estate
State of **Oregon**   County of **Multnomah**

BEFORE ME, the undersigned authority, on this day personally appeared Joe Seller AND Jane Seller, who being first duly sworn, deposes and says that:

1. A ___Purchase and Sale Agreement or ___ Option agreement of the real property described in the attached Exhibit "A" was entered into by and between the Affiant, as Buyer, and Joe Seller AND Jane Seller, as Seller, on the ___ day of _____, 200__.

2. The closing of the purchase and sale of said real property, per the terms of the Agreement, is to take place on or before the ___ day of _____, 20___.

A copy of the agreement for purchase and sale of said real property may be obtained by contacting Joe Investor, whose mailing address is 233 Smith Street, Vancouver, WA 99008 , and whose telephone number is 360-999-1000.

LEGAL: 5th Block of the last piece of dirt in Portland

Property Address: 555 Forest street, Portland, OR 99889

X_____ X_____ Date_____ ,200__
Joe Seller   **AFFIANT Joe Investor**

X_____
Jane Seller

State of _____   County of _____
I Hereby Certify that on this day, before me, an officer duly authorized in the State of _____ aforesaid to take acknowledgments, personally appeared Joe Seller AND Jane Seller to me known as the person(s) described in and who executed the foregoing instrument and Acknowledged before me that he / she executed the same. Witness my hand and official seal in the county and State last aforesaid this ___ day of _____, 200__

X_____NotaryPublic   My commission expires_____

State of _____   County of _____

I Hereby Certify that on this day, before me, an officer duly authorized in the State of _____ aforesaid to take acknowledgments, personally appeared Joe Investor to me known as the person(s) described in and who executed the foregoing instrument and Acknowledged before me that he / she executed the same. Witness my hand and official seal in the county and State last aforesaid this
____day of_____, 200__

x_____Notary Public   My commission expires_____

OPTION TO PURCHASE REAL ESTATE AGREEMENT

THIS AGREEMENT is made and entered into this _____ day of _____, **200__** by and between **Joe Seller** AND **Jane Seller** and all title holders to the property (hereinafter referred to as "Optionor"), and **Joe Investor** (hereinafter referred to as "Optionee").

WITNESSETH THAT, under the mutual promises and covenants hereinafter set forth, the parties hereto agree as follows:

      1. **OPTION TO PURCHASE REAL PROPERTY**: Optionor grants unto Optionee the exclusive right to purchase the real property described below (legal description is attached as exhibit "A", annexed hereto).

      Address: 555 Forest street, Portland, OR 99889

      LEGAL: 5th Block of the last piece of dirt in Portland

      2. **TERM OF OPTION**: The term of the Option shall be for a period of _____ months, commencing on the ___ day of _____, 20___, and expiring on the _____ day of _____, 20___.

      3. **OPTION PRICE**: Optionee shall have the right to purchase the Property for $_____ (_____DOLLARS), until the exercising of this Option, to be paid per Terms of Sale contained herein. Unless otherwise stated herein, Optionee shall pay closing costs as per the executed Standard Real Estate Purchase and Sale Agreement

      4. **TERMS OF SALE:** The terms of sale shall be:
_____
_____

_____
_____

_____
_____

All personal property, appliances, attachments and fixtures shall be included in said sale except:

_____

_____

1. **OPTION CONSIDERATION:** In exchange for this Option, Optionee agrees to pay Optionor the payment of $ _____ (_____ **Dollars)** concurrent with the inception of this Option Agreement, and other good and valuable consideration in hand paid to Optionor, the receipt and sufficiency whereof are hereby acknowledged by Optionor.

2. **EXTENSION OF OPTION PERIOD:** Upon payment of $ _____, Optionee shall have the right to extend this option by _____ months under the same terms and conditions.

3. **NOTICE OF EXERCISE:** This option may be exercised at any time during the option period as described above, and Optionee may exercise said option with or without notice to Optionor.

4. **ESCROW OF CLOSING DOCUMENTS:** All documents necessary for title transfer, including, but not limited to a warranty deed and bill of sale, shall be executed and held in escrow with an escrow agent of Optionee's choosing. Optionor shall execute a deed of trust or mortgage in favor of Optionee to secure performance of this agreement.

5. **MAINTENANCE AND REPAIRS:** Optionee acknowledges that the premises are in acceptable order and repair, unless otherwise indicated herein. Unless otherwise agreed, Optionor shall, at his own expense, and at all times, maintain the premises in a clean and sanitary manner, including all equipment and appliances therein and shall surrender the same, at the exercising of this Agreement, in good condition, normal wear and tear excepted. Should Optionor fail to maintain and repair Property in accordance with this provision, Optionee shall have the option to make said repairs and be credited under the provisions of Paragraph 13.

6. **INSURANCE:** Optionor shall protect Optionee's interest by maintaining hazard insurance upon the property, naming the Optionee as additional insured. In the event of destruction in whole or in part of the property, Optionee shall have the option to proceed with the closing and accept the insurance proceeds for said damage, or to declare this agreement null and void, releasing both parties from any obligations hereunder, except for the return of monies paid by Optionee which shall become immediately due and payable from the insurance proceeds.

7. **TAXES:** Optionor shall timely pay all city and county taxes, and any other assessments, or association fees or other fees, which may become due during the term of this Option Agreement. Should Optionor fail to pay said taxes, assessments or fees in accordance with this provision, Optionee shall have the option to pay said taxes, assessments or fees and be credited under the provisions of Paragraph 13.

8. **OTHER ENCUMBRANCES:** Optionor representing that the following liens and encumbrances currently exist on the property:

_____

_____

_____

_____

Optionor covenants that he will not further impair or encumber the property without Optionee's express written permission. In the event Optionor defaults on the payment of any of said security instruments, Optionee shall have the right to cure and/or satisfy said security instruments, and, in this event, shall be entitled to a 18% interest on actual expenses incurred in doing so.

9. **ASSIGNMENT:** Optionee shall be permitted the right of assignment of this option.

10. **PURCHASE AND SALE AGREEMENT:** In the event of the exercise of this Option by Optionee, Optionor binds himself to enter into a "Purchase and Sale Agreement", attached hereto as Exhibit "B" and made part a hereof by reference, with Optionee. In the absence of a Purchase and Sale Agreement, the closing agent may use this Option Agreement as the contract to close on.

11. **AGREEMENT BINDING:** This Agreement shall be binding upon the parties hereto and their respective heirs, administrators, successors, and assigns.

12. **SPECIFIC PERFORMANCE:** Optionor herewith certifies and warrants that he/she is vested with full powers and authority to enter into this Agreement. In addition to the remedies specified herein, Optionee may, in the event of default by Optionor, enforce this agreement through an action for specific performance with the attorney fees and costs of said action being paid by Optionor.

13. **CANCELLATION FEE:** Optionor may request the right to cancel this agreement by paying $_____ ("cancellation fee") to

Optionee. Upon receipt of Cancellation Fee, Optionee agrees to execute any documents needed to relinquish any further interest in the subject property.

14. **GOVERNING LAW:** This agreement, and all transactions contemplated hereby, shall be governed by, construed and enforced in accordance with the laws of the State of **Oregon**. The parties herein waive trial by jury and agree to submit to the personal jurisdiction and venue of a court of subject matter jurisdiction located in **Multnomah** County, State of **Oregon**. In the event that litigation results from or arises out of this Agreement or the performance thereof, the parties agree to reimburse the prevailing party's reasonable attorney's fees, court costs, and all other expenses, whether or not declared by the court as costs, in addition to any other relief to which the prevailing party may be entitled. In such event, no action shall be entertained by said court or any court of competent jurisdiction if filed more than one year subsequent to the date the cause(s) of action actually accrued regardless of whether damages were otherwise as of said time calculable.

15. **TIME:** Time is of the essence of this Option Agreement.

16. **SEVERABILITY:** In the event any part of this Option Agreement be construed as unenforceable, the remaining parts of this Agreement shall remain in full force and effect as though the unenforceable part or parts were not written into this Option Agreement.

17. **GENDER:** All references to Optionor or Optionee herein employed shall be construed to include the plural as well as the singular, and the masculine shall include the feminine and neuter where the context of this Agreement may require.

18. **ACCESS:** Current owner of record will permit Optionee to hold an event to attract as many potential buyers as possible during the agreed upon option period. Optionor understands that a significant amount of resources are being committed to the project and Optionor will not obstruct Optionee's event in any way during the agreed upon Optioned period.

ADDITIONAL TERMS:

_____

_____

19. **ENTIRE AGREEMENT:** This Agreement and any attached addendum constitutes the sole and entire Agreement between the parties and no representation, promise, or inducement not included in this Agreement, oral or written, shall be binding upon any party hereto.

IN WITNESS WHEREOF, the parties have signed this Agreement the day and year first above written. If more than one party is shown as Optionor or Optionee, and should less than all sign, then the party or parties signing warrant they are acting as agent to sign for any party not signing this Agreement. As to Optionor, signed, sealed and delivered in the presence of:

X_____ _____,200__ X_____ _____, 200__
Optionor   **Joe Seller**   **Joe Investor**

X_____ _____, 200__
Optionor   **Jane Seller**

EXHIBIT "A"

Property address:

555 Forest street, Portland, OR 99889

Legal description:

5th Block of the last piece of dirt in Portland

Assignment of Contract
For Purchase and Sale or an Option

In reference to the contract for purchase and sale dated _____,
200__ between _____ **Joe Seller** AND **Jane Seller** as __ Seller
___Optionor and **Joe Investor** as __ Buyer ___Optionee, concerning property
described as (legal):

5th Block of the last piece of dirt in Portland

Street Address: **555 Forest street, Portland, OR 99889**

Joe Investor as Assignor hereby assigns all rights to said contract for sale and

purchase to **Ken Retailer** as Assignee, in exchange for compensation in the amount

of **$7,000** . A non refundable binder of **$1,000** is made this date, and shall be only

be credit and deducted at closing, as a credit against the assignment fee due upon

closing. Said closing shall occur on or before _____, 200__, or this

assignment expires and binder payment forfeited by assignee.

Further, this fee is payable as a demand against any future escrow of subject

property.

X_____   _____, 200__
Assignor: **Joe Investor**

X_____   _____,200__

Assignee: **Ken Retailer**

State of _____   County of _____

I Hereby Certify that on this day, before me, an officer duly authorized in the State
of _____ aforesaid to take acknowledgments, personally appeared **Joe**
Investor as assignor to me known as the person(s) described in and who executed

the foregoing instrument and Acknowledged before me that **he / she / they** executed the same.

Witness my hand and official seal in the county and State last aforesaid this ___**day of** _____, 200__

x_____
Notary Public
My commission expires_____
State of _____   County of _____

I Hereby Certify that on this day, before me, an officer duly authorized in the State of _____ aforesaid to take acknowledgments, personally appeared **Ken Retailer as assignee** to me known as the person(s) described in and who executed the foregoing instrument and Acknowledged before me that **he / she / they** executed the same.

Witness my hand and official seal in the county and State last aforesaid this ___**day of** _____, 200__

x_____
Notary Public
My commission expires____

Definition of "Equity" and your Selling Options

Realistic possible fast sale price for an investor $_____

Realtor/conventional sale		**Rental**	
Fee 6%	$_____	Vacancy rate 25%	_____
Closing costs	$_____	Damages	$_____
Payments	$_____	Landlord court	_____
Repairs required	$_____	Pets/other occupants	_____
Repairs desired	$_____	Emergency repairs	_____
Vested interest?	Y / N		

Make your payments?   Y / N
Is this what you WANT?   Y / N

Total costs   - $_____

Payoffs   - $_____

Real Equity $_____

Is this what you WANT?   Y / N

Our Solution

No repairs ? ___
Flexible ? ___
Gets you the result you need ? _____
Solve the main problems ? ___
Solve all of your problems? ___(likely not ALL)
Payments taken care of ? ___
Timely? ___
Fewer worries? ___
Vested interest ? ___
Best solution so you can move on now ?
___

Our solution/offer :

_____

_____

_____

_____

Seller Initials _____ _____   **Asset Solutions 2100, LLC - T.J. Marrs   360-883-2296   tjmarrs@creclub.com**

Grantor/Seller Joe Seller & Jane Seller
Address: 123 Anywhere street, Omaha, NB 99889

Grantee/Buyer
Joe Investor
Address: 233 Smith street, Vancouver, WA 99008

After recording return to: Joe Investor
233 Smith street, Vancouver, WA 99008

Send all tax statements to: Joe Investor
233 Smith street, Vancouver, WA 99008

STATE OF Oregon
COUNTY OF Multnomah

I certify that within
instrument ws received for record
on_____, 200__
at _____ o'clock ___M., and
recorded in book/reel/volume No.
_____ on page
_____ and/or as
fee/file/instrument/microfilm/ reception No.
_____, Records of said
County.

Witnessed my hand and seal of County affixed.

_____
Name   Title

By, _____, Deputy.

WARRANTY DEED

THIS DEED, made this ___ day of _____, 20__ between **Joe Seller and Jane Seller** the grantor, whose address is **123 Anywhere street, Omaha, NB   99889** and **Joe Investor** the grantee, whose address is **233 Smith street, Vancouver, WA 99008.**

WITNESSETH, that the grantor, for and in consideration of the sum of **ONE HUNDRED** DOLLARS (**$100**), the receipt and sufficiency of which is hereby acknowledged and received, and for other good and valuable consideration, has granted bargained, sold and conveyed, and by these presents does grant, bargain sell, convey and confirm unto the grantee, their heirs and assigns forever, all the real property, together with improvements, if any, situate and being in the County of **Multnomah**, State of **Oregon**, described as follows:

5th Block of the last piece of dirt in Portland

Also known as street and number: **555 Forest street, Portland, OR 99889**

TOGETHER with all and singular hereditaments and appurtenances thereunto belonging, or in anywise appertaining and the reversion and reversions, remainder and remainders, rents, issues, and profits thereof, and all the estate, right, title, interest, claim and demand whatsoever of the said grantor, either in law or equity, of, in and to the above bargained premises, with the hereditaments and appurtenances.

TO HAVE AND TO HOLD the said premises above bargained and described, with the appurtenances, unto the said grantee, their heirs and assigns forever. And the said grantor, for himself, his heirs, and personal representatives, does covenant, grant bargain and agree to and with the grantee, their heirs and assigns, that at the time of the ensealing and delivery of these presents, is well seized of the premises above conveyed, has good, sure, perfect, absolute indefeasible estate if inheritance, in law, in fee simple, and has good right, full power and lawful authority to grant, bargain, sell and convey the same in manner and form aforesaid, and that the same are free and clear from all former and other grants, bargains, sales, liens, taxes, assessments, encumbrances and restrictions of any kind or nature whatsoever, except any easements, restrictions, covenants, zoning ordinances

and rights-of-way of record and property taxes accruing subsequent to
_____, 20___ , a lien not yet due and payable.

The grantor shall and will WARRANT AND FOREVER DEFEND the above-bargained premises in the quiet and peaceable possession of the grantee, his heirs, and assigns, against all and every person or persons lawfully claiming the whole or any part thereof. The singular shall include the plural, the plural shall include the singular, and the use of any gender shall be applicable to all genders.

IN WITNESS WHEREOF, the grantor has executed this deed on the date set forth above.

x_____   _____, 20__
Joe Seller

x_____   _____, 20__
Jane Seller

STATE OF _____ COUNTY OF _____
On _____, 20 ___ , before me, _____ , a notary public in and for said state personally appeared **Joe Seller and Jane Seller** , personally known to me (or proved to me based upon satisfactory evidence) to be the person(s) whose name(s) are subscribed to the within instrument and acknowledged that (s)he/they executed the same in his/her/their signature on the instrument the person(s) or entity on behalf of which they acted, executed the instrument.

Witness my hand and official seal

x_____
NOTARY PUBLIC
My commission expires _____

NOTICE TO THE BUYER

THE FOLLOWING DISCLOSURES ARE MADE BY THE SELLER(S), CONCERNING THE CONDITION OF THE PROPERTY LOCATED AT . . . . _____

("THE PROPERTY"), OR AS LEGALLY DESCRIBED ON ATTACHED EXHIBIT A.

DISCLOSURES CONTAINED IN THIS FORM ARE PROVIDED BY THE SELLER ON THE BASIS OF SELLER'S ACTUAL KNOWLEDGE OF THE PROPERTY AT THE TIME THIS DISCLOSURE FORM IS COMPLETED BY THE SELLER. YOU HAVE THREE BUSINESS DAYS, UNLESS OTHERWISE AGREED, FROM THE SELLER'S DELIVERY OF THIS SELLER'S DISCLOSURE STATEMENT TO RESCIND YOUR AGREEMENT BY DELIVERING YOUR SEPARATE SIGNED WRITTEN STATEMENT OF RESCISSION TO THE SELLER, UNLESS YOU WAIVE THIS RIGHT AT OR PRIOR TO ENTERING INTO A SALE AGREEMENT. THE FOLLOWING ARE DISCLOSURES MADE BY THE SELLER AND ARE NOT THE REPRESENTATIONS OF ANY REAL ESTATE LICENSEE OR OTHER PARTY. THIS INFORMATION IS FOR DISCLOSURE ONLY AND IS NOT INTENDED TO BE A PART OF ANY WRITTEN AGREEMENT BETWEEN THE BUYER AND THE SELLER.

FOR A MORE COMPREHENSIVE EXAMINATION OF THE SPECIFIC CONDITION OF THIS PROPERTY YOU ARE ADVISED TO OBTAIN AND PAY FOR THE SERVICES OF A QUALIFIED SPECIALIST TO INSPECT THE PROPERTY ON YOUR BEHALF, FOR EXAMPLE, ARCHITECTS, ENGINEERS, LAND SURVEYORS, PLUMBERS, ELECTRICIANS, ROOFERS, BUILDING INSPECTORS, OR PEST AND DRY ROT INSPECTORS. THE PROSPECTIVE BUYER AND THE OWNER MAY WISH TO OBTAIN PROFESSIONAL ADVICE OR INSPECTIONS OF THE PROPERTY AND TO PROVIDE FOR APPROPRIATE PROVISIONS IN A CONTRACT BETWEEN THEM WITH RESPECT TO ANY ADVICE, INSPECTION, DEFECTS OR WARRANTIES.

Seller ___ is ___ is not occupying the property.

I. SELLER'S DISCLOSURES: *If "Yes" attach a copy or explain. If necessary use an attached sheet.

1. **TITLE**

___Yes ___No ___Don't know   A. Do you have legal authority to sell the property?

___Yes ___No ___Don't know   B. Is title to the property subject to any of the following?

(1) First right of refusal ___ (2) Option ___ (3) Lease or rental agreement ___ (4) Life estate? ___

___Yes ___No ___Don't know   *C. Are there any encroachments, boundary agreements, or boundary disputes?

___Yes ___No ___Don't know   *D. Are there any rights of way, easements, or access limitations that may affect the owner's use of the property?

___Yes ___No ___Don't know   E. Are there any written agreements for joint maintenance of an easement or right of way?

___Yes ___No ___Don't know   F. Is there any study, survey project, or notice that would adversely affect the property?

___Yes ___No ___Don't know   G. Are there any pending or existing assessments against the property?

___Yes ___No ___Don't know   H. Are there any zoning violations, nonconforming uses, or any unusual restrictions on the subject property that would affect future construction or remodeling?

___Yes ___No ___Don't know   I. Is there a boundary survey for the property?

___Yes ___No ___Don't know   J. Are there any covenants, conditions, or restrictions which affect the property?

WATER:

A. Household Water Private [ ] Shared   1) The source of the water is [ ] Public [ ] Community [ ]

2) Water source information:

___Yes ___No ___Don't know   a. Are there any written agreements for shared water source?

___Yes ___No ___Don't know   b. Is there an easement (recorded or unrecorded) for access to and/or maintenance of the water source?

___Yes ___No ___Don't know   c. Are any known problems or repairs needed?

___Yes ___No ___Don't know   d. Does the source provide an adequate year round supply of potable water?

___Yes ___No ___Don't know   e. Are there any water treatment systems for the property? [ ]Leased [ ]Owned

B.   Irrigation

___Yes ___No ___Don't know   1) Are there any water rights for the property?

___Yes ___No ___Don't know   2) If they exist, to your knowledge, have the water rights been used during the last five-year period?

___Yes ___No ___Don't know   3) If so, is the certificate available?

3.   SEWER/SEPTIC SYSTEM

A. The property is served by: [ ] Public sewer main   [ ] Septic tank system   [ ] Other disposal system (describe)_____

___Yes ___No ___Don't know   B. If the property is served by a public or community sewer main, is the house connected to   the main?

___Yes ___No ___Don't know   C. Is the property currently subject to a sewer capacity charge?

___Yes ___No ___Don't know   D. If the property is connected to a septic system

___Yes ___No ___Don't know   1) Was a permit issued for its construction, and was it approved by the city or county following its construction?

___Don't know   (2) When was it last pumped: _____,

_____

___Yes ___No ___Don't know   (3) Are there any defects in the operation of the septic system?

___Don't know   (4) When was it last inspected? _____, _____

___Yes ___No ___Don't know   5) How many bedrooms was the system approved for?
_____ BR

___Yes ___No ___Don't know   E. Do all plumbing fixtures, including laundry drain, go to the septic/sewer system? If no, explain:

_____

___Yes ___No ___Don't know   F. Are you aware of any changes or repairs to the septic system?

___Yes ___No ___Don't know   G. Is the septic tank system, including the drain field, located entirely within the boundaries of the property?

4.   STRUCTURAL

___Yes ___No ___Don't know   A. Has the roof leaked?   If yes, has it been repaired? _____

___Yes ___No ___Don't know   B. Have there been any conversions, additions, or remodeling?

___Yes ___No ___Don't know   1. If yes, were all building permits obtained?

___Yes ___No ___Don't know   2. If yes, were all final inspections obtained?

___Yes ___No ___Don't know   C. Do you know the age of the house? If yes, year of original construction: _____

___Yes ___No ___Don't know   D. Do you know of any settling, slippage, or sliding of either the house or other   structures/improvements located on the property? If yes, explain: _____

___Yes ___No ___Don't know   E. Do you know of any defects with the following: (Please check applicable items)

    ___Foundation ___Decks ___Walls ___Chimneys
    ___Interior Walls ___Alarm ___Doors ___Windows
    ___Patios ___Ceilings ___Slab floors ___Drive ways
    ___Pool ___Hot tub ___Sauna ___Sidewalk
    ___Outbuildings ___Fire places ___Floors ___Walkways
    ___Other _____ ___Wood stoves

___Yes ___No ___Don't know   F. Was a pest or dry rot, structural or "whole house" inspection done?   When and by whom was the   inspection completed?
_____

___Yes ___No ___Don't know   G. Since assuming ownership, has your property had a problem with wood destroying organisms   and/or have there been any problems with pest control, infestations, or vermin?

5.   SYSTEMS AND FIXTURES   If the following systems or fixtures are included with the transfer, do they have any existing defects:

___Yes ___No ___Don't know   A. Electrical system, including wiring, switches, outlets, and service

___Yes ___No ___Don't know   B. Plumbing system, including pipes, faucets, fixtures, and toilets

___Yes ___No ___Don't know   C. Hot water tank

___Yes ___No ___Don't know   D. Garbage disposal

___Yes ___No ___Don't know   E. Appliances

___Yes ___No ___Don't know   F. Sump pump

___Yes ___No ___Don't know   G. Heating and cooling systems

___Yes ___No ___Don't know   H. Security system

___Yes ___No ___Don't know   [ ] Owned   [ ] Leased   [ ] Other

6. COMMON INTEREST

___Yes ___No ___Don't know   A. Is there a Home Owners' Association? Name of Association

___Yes ___No ___Don't know   B. Are there regular periodic assessments:
$_____ per [ ] Month [ ] Year [ ] Other

___Yes ___No ___Don't know   C. Are there any pending special assessments?

___Yes ___No ___Don't know   D. Are there any shared "common areas" or any joint maintenance agreements (facilities such as walls, fences, landscaping, pools, tennis courts, walkways, or other areas co-owned in undivided interest with others)?

7. GENERAL

___Yes ___No ___Don't know   A. Is there any settling, soil, standing water, or drainage problems on the property?

___Yes ___No ___Don't know   B. Does the property contain fill material?

___Yes ___No ___Don't know   C. Is there any material damage to the property or any of the structure from fire, wind, floods, beach   movements, earthquake, expansive soils, or landslides?

___Yes ___No ___Don't know   D. Is the property in a designated flood plain?

___Yes ___No ___Don't know   E. Are there any substances, materials, or products that may be an environmental hazard such as, but not limited to, asbestos, formaldehyde, radon gas, lead-based paint, fuel or chemical storage tanks, and contaminated soil or water on the subject property?

___Yes ___No ___Don't know   F. Are there any tanks or underground storage tanks (e.g., chemical, fuel, etc.) on the property?

___Yes ___No ___Don't know   G. Has the property ever been used as an illegal drug manufacturing site?

8. FULL DISCLOSURE BY SELLERS

A. Other conditions or defects:

___Yes ___No ___Don't know   Are there any other material defects affecting this property or its value that a prospective buyer should know about?

B. Verification:

___Yes ___No ___Don't know   The foregoing answers and attached explanations (if any) are complete and correct to the best of my/our knowledge and I/we have received a copy hereof. I/we authorize all of my/our real estate licensees, if any, to deliver a copy of this disclosure statement to other real estate licensees and all prospective buyers of the property.

_____   _____   _____
seller   Seller   Date

II   BUYER'S ACKNOWLEDGMENT

A.   As buyer(s), I/we acknowledge the duty to pay diligent attention to any material defects which are known to me/us or can be known to me/us by utilizing diligent attention and observation.

B.   Each buyer acknowledges and understands that the disclosures set forth in this statement and in any amendments to this statement are made only by the seller.

C.   Buyer (which term includes all persons signing the "buyer's acceptance" portion of this disclosure statement below) hereby acknowledges receipt of a copy of this disclosure statement (including attachments, if any) bearing seller's signature.

DISCLOSURES CONTAINED IN THIS FORM ARE PROVIDED BY THE SELLER ON THE BASIS OF SELLER'S ACTUAL KNOWLEDGE OF THE PROPERTY AT THE TIME OF DISCLOSURE. YOU, THE BUYER, HAVE THREE BUSINESS DAYS, UNLESS OTHERWISE AGREED, FROM THE SELLER'S DELIVERY OF THIS SELLER'S DISCLOSURE STATEMENT TO RESCIND YOUR AGREEMENT BY DELIVERING YOUR SEPARATE SIGNED WRITTEN STATEMENT OF RESCISSION TO THE SELLER UNLESS YOU WAIVE THIS RIGHT OF RESCISSION. BUYER HEREBY ACKNOWLEDGES RECEIPT OF A COPY OF THIS REAL PROPERTY TRANSFER DISCLOSURE STATEMENT AND ACKNOWLEDGES THAT THE DISCLOSURES MADE HEREIN ARE THOSE OF THE SELLER ONLY, AND NOT OF ANY REAL ESTATE LICENSEE OR OTHER PARTY.

BUYER _____**BUYER** _____**Date**_____, 200__

Sample Real Estate Business Plan

Objective: To build an outstanding real estate portfolio. My goals for the business are to first generate immediate income for bills and debt reduction, and second to build a successful real estate business in order to accumulate capital and credit to support my lifestyle and other investment opportunities or business ventures.

Commitment:

- To help alleviate the real estate problems others
- To help qualified people become home owners
- Minimum 15 hours per week in the business (including all day Fridays and half Saturday)
    - Learning and implementing marketing strategies
    - Calling on sellers a minimum of 1 hour twice a week
    - Minimum of 4 hours per week education

Monetary:

- Individual Goals:
    - $1,500 of monthly residual income from real estate by end of 2003
    - $60,000 cash from real estate for 2004 (reevaluate 6 months; $2,500 monthly)

- o $120,000 cash in 2007 (minimum $5,000 monthly residual income)

- Additional Partnership Goals:
    - o Minimum 6 deals completed by 8/31/04
    - o Net profit/equity in partnership of $60,000 (ave. $10,000 per deal; does not include rental income, tax deductions)
    - o 10 Deals in Year 2 (consider adding staff)
    - o 12 Deals in Year 3
    - o $400,000 equity by end of Year 5

Structure

- I will be the driver of my business, doing the leg work and making decisions/recommendations

- I plan to use partners to help grow my business more quickly and allow me to do transactions that I may not be able to do on my own (i.e. require capital or credit)

- May add other corporations/pieces to segregate for tax and liability considerations

- Will likely eventually integrate with other businesses to leverage resources and maximize tax benefits

- Would also like to give family/friends opportunity to work into the business in the future perhaps with their separate arm/corporations

Marketing

Budget:

- $250 for start up and October marketing
- Minimum $50-100 per month through end of 2003 (depending on cash flow)
- Reevaluate budget and advertising methods for January 2004

Initial Strategies:

- Business cards
- Driving for $
- Classified Ads
- Direct mail
- Networking
- Signs
- Divorce/Probate records
- Door Hangers / Fliers
- Expired MLS listings
- Website

Considerations

❖ Need to focus on ways to generate income quickly

❖ I may need some help with Marketing (financial and ideas/strategies) in the beginning

❖ Must make time to focus on new company (Geis Asset Management)

Education

❖ Focus on improving marketing skills

❖ Develop target areas for marketing

❖ Practice phoning to sellers and handling objections

❖ Become proficient at 'Subject to' transactions

❖ Must become more familiar with internet tools (i.e. auto-responders, advertising)

❖ Asset protection strategies for myself, and particularly at this stage, my business partners

Next Steps

➢ Complete closing on current properties

- One on contract (currently refinancing) which is cash flowing at ~$80 per month (with about $10K equity; $21K purchase – $32K appraised value) – possible lease option when lease expires December

- Second will cash flow at ~$500 per month (Section 8)

- Print business cards (Kinko's ?) by 9/26/03
- Start "WE BUY HOUSES" Ad campaign in classifieds 9/25/03
- Incorporate other tactics in following weeks
    - Letters and follow up to divorce/probate leads 10/3/03
    - Begin with direct mail 10/10/03 (determine target areas)
    - Begin marketing for qualified buyers with first leads
    - Learn and utilize internet marketing tools/strategies
- Continue establishing birddogs and other resources (attys., realtors, ect.)

Printed in the United States
67896LVS00004B/130-177

9 781598 002126